ALI SHARIATI

RELIGION
vs
RELIGION

TRANSLATED FROM THE PERSIAN BY
LALEH BAKHTIAR

FOREWORD BY
ANDREW BURGESS

Library of Congress Cataloging-in-Publication Data

Shariati, Ali (1933-1977)
Religion vs. Religion

1. Religion 2. Islam   I. Title II. Shariati, Ali

ISBN 1-871031-001-1 (pbk)

Published by
ABC International Group, Inc
Distributed by
Kazi Publications
3023 W. Belmont Ave Chicago IL 60618
(T) (773) 267-7001; (F) (773) 267-7002
email: info@kazi.org www. kazi.org

CONTENTS

Foreword   5
Introduction   11
Lecture One:
Introduction   19
    Kufr (Denying the Truth)   23
    Multitheism (*shirk*)   24
    Idolism   24
    Monotheism (*tawhid*)   26
Preventing the Spread of Monotheism   27
    The Samaritan   28
    Balaam   28
    The Pharisees   28
The Paradox   29
    What does a religion of revolution mean?   31
    What does a religion of legitimation mean? 32
    Commanding to Good and Preventing Evil   32
The Continuation of Multitheism   32
The Roots of the Religion of Multitheism   34
    Ownership of a Minority
    Over an Abased Majority   34

Legitimation of the Status Quo   34
Promotion of Class Superiority   35
Narcosis or Inner Surrender   35
Withholding Responsibility   35
The Movement of Multitheism:
Manifest and Hidden   35
Conclusion   39

Lecture Two:
Introduction   43
Kufr vs. Islam   45
Religion in Ancient Iran   50
    The First and Second Class   50
    The Third Class   50
    The Magi Legitimate Class Differences   51
Multitheism   53
The Intellectuals' Error   56
The Mission of Intellectuals and Ulama 57
Conclusion   59
Endnotes to Lecture Two   64
Glossary   65
Index   71

Foreword
On Drawing a Line

Reflecting on his experience as an engraver, William Blake once remarked that, in art as in life, the decisive factor is how you draw a line. "What is it that distinguishes honesty from knavery, but the hard and wiry line of rectitude and certainty in the actions and intentions? Leave out this line, and you leave out life itself; all is chaos again, and the line of the almighty must be drawn out upon it before man or beast can exist." [1]

It is a long way from Blake, the eighteenth century English artist and poet to Ali Shariati, the twentieth century Iranian sociologist and Islamologist; yet not impossibly far. For, despite their differences, the two share a moral passion leading them to draw lines in their writings calling for religious and social reform. A reader may not like where or how a line cuts, but there it is, bold and uncompromising, leaving one no choice but to stand on one side or the other.

The line Shariati draws in the following speeches is between two religions, a "religion of revolution" and a "religion of legitimation." The difference between them is sharply drawn: the first is a religion working to overcome differences in class and economic status, while the second is a religion legitimating and perpetuating such differences. As opposed to some socialists who draw the line between religion, as supporter of class divisions, and non-religion, which overcomes these divisions, he places the dividing-line within religion itself. From his perspective, it is thus not religion itself that needs to be rejected as the "opium of the people," but only one type of religion, the "religion of legitimation," while true religion remains unscathed.

The consequences of this impressive analysis are far-reaching. Not for nothing has he been called the ideological leader of Iran's "Islamic Revolution." Since World War II the Muslim world has been shaken by two powerful forces, socialist ideology and, more recently, what is now called Islamic fundamentalism. The line Shariati draws binds these two movements together: true Islam, he says, is true socialism, and true socialism is true Islam. It is the kind of slogan for which thousands of people have been prepared to die, and for which thousands have already died.

Shariati's designation as a "sociologist" will be puzzling to American readers, who are accustomed to an academic science of sociology claiming to be descriptive rather than ideological. Certainly one looks at his pages in vain for the charts of statistical correlations that characterize American sociology. His life, also, shows as much of political activism as of academic detachment. Born in 1933, he early joined the "Socialist Movement of Believers-in-God" and by the 1950's he was already active in the movement for the nationalization of the Iranian oil industry. When he earned his B.A. in French and Persian in 1958 and left for graduate study in France at the Sorbonne, his double mission continued. His doctoral dissertation (1963) was a translation into French of a medieval Persian text. During this same period, however, he also translated into Persian Ernesto "Che" Guevara, Jean Paul Sartre, and Franz Fanon, and he helped found the Freedom Movement of Iran, Abroad. On his return to Iran in 1964 he was jailed for six months. From then on he held various teaching positions until he was sent into forced retirement in 1969. In 1972 he was arrested for his activities, and he was not released until an international outcry compelled the government to give him his freedom in 1975. For the next two years he was under house arrest. In 1977 he left Iran for England, where he died under mysterious circumstances in a relative's home. Clearly this was not the typical life of a professor of sociology. [2]

The key to Shariati's understanding of sociology is to be found in his affinity with Guevara, Fanon, and Sartre. Both of the first two took active part in a socialist struggle - Guevara in Latin America, and Fanon in Algeria; and even the more professorial Sartre found himself frequently under arrest in France for political demonstrations. Like Karl Marx, all of these men felt called upon not just to understand the world but to change it.

But if Shariati is an unorthodox sociologist, he is just as unorthodox as a Marxist socialist. The "Socialist Movement of Believers-in-God" differed from Marx in much more than their belief in God. Their faith was rooted in a literal interpretation of the Quran as the Word of God, a basis that puts them at odds with Marxism from the start. Classical Marxism, which begins as a kind of Christian heresy, does not quite know how to account for Islam. By Marxist theory the ideal state is not supposed to be proclaimed in the Arabian deserts during the seventh century A.D., and a proletarian revolution should not erupt there either.

In many respects, Shariati's nearest allies are to be found not among the secular European socialists, whom he frequently cites, but among the Latin American Christian "liberation theologians," of whom he does not seem to be aware. Some of these liberation theologians, such as Camilo Torres (Columbia), Carlos Alberto ("Frei Betto"), Libanio Christo (Brazil), and Gustavo Gutierrez (Peru), were beginning to attract world notice by 1970, the year in which Shariati gave the following speeches. [3]   Other liberation theologians include Juan Luis Segundo (Uruguay), Hugo Assmann (Brazil), Elsa Tamez (Costa Rica), Jose Miguez Bonino (Argentina), Jose Porfirio Miranda (Mexico), Ernesto Cardenal (Nicaragua), Dom Helder Camara (Brazil), and Leonardo and Cleodovis Boff (Brazil). Several of these, or their followers, suffered imprisonment or death. It would not be stretching the term to call them all socialist "Believers-in-God". Like Shariati, they have held passionately to their faith and its social consequences, at the same time as they have felt free to deviate from classical socialist teachings at many points.

The closest analogue to Shariati among the Latin American liberation theologians comes in Enrique Dussel's historical analysis of the colonial expansion by European powers. [4] In his history of the church in Latin America, Dussel uses a hermeneutical model based on a division between the oppressors and the oppressed. Since both oppressors and oppressed claim to interpret their actions in religious terms, the way the line is drawn between them is strikingly reminiscent of Shariati's division between the two kinds of religion.

The Western reader of this book may be surprised at the way in which Shariati draws his main harsh examples of oppression out of religions remote from Islamic Iran, such as Greek polytheism, Christianity (especially medieval Catholicism), Judaism (in the person of its leaders, the Pharisees or rabbis), Zoroastrianism, and occasionally other religions such as Buddhism. This practice may well puzzle readers, who will wonder how a critique of false religion described in terms of an attack on Zoroastrianism or Christianity is to be understood as a call to social revolution in Iran today. Surely, such readers would say, we cannot suppose that his Iranian listeners were in danger of succumbing to the lures of Christianity, for example, especially medieval Christianity, or that they needed to be warned against the social structure it is supposed to represent. Indeed, one can hardly suppose that if his Iranian audience had any real familiarity with non-Muslim faiths they would have been satisfied with some of the characterizations provided. Why then should a critique mainly of non-Islamic faiths and their social structures be taken - as in fact it was - as a call for change in contemporary Iran?

Part of the problem here might be overcome through a wider acquaintance with Shariati's writings. Although his productivity is enormous, scores of his writings have not been translated in any language and only a few have been translated into English. At the conclusion of his meditational work, *Hajj: Reflections on its Rituals*, for example, he points out how even these rituals at the heart of Islam have sometimes been deceptively twisted around to serve false religion. In another book, *Alid Shi'ism/Safavid Shi'ism*, [5] he criticizes tendencies within his own branch of Islam. Through such writings, he has gained a reputation in Iran as a relentless critic of false religion within the Islamic tradition itself.

An equally important factor is the political situation in Iran when these speeches are delivered. In 1970 the struggle with the Shah is well underway, and there are certain criticisms of the existing society that dare not be uttered in public. His Iranian listeners, however, are able to de-code easily what he says. They are aware, much better than Europeans or Americans would be, that the confrontation between Ali and his opponents described in these speeches was not the end of the struggle within Islam between the kind of religion calling for revolution and the kind of religion legitimating oppression. His listeners know Islamic history - of the opulent lives led by the Baghdad caliphs described in the "Arabian Nights," while the common people groaned in poverty; of wars of conquest in the name of Allah; of peoples dragged off into slavery, the men slaughtered or put to forced labor, the women thrown into harems; of oppression in terms of race and of class, all justified in their day by those who claimed to be Muslim mullahs. That is why Shariati's speeches can be understood as calls to revolution. Behind the stories of oppression in Europe and pre-Muslim Iran, the listeners can hear their own.

Indeed, Shariati's own life fills in what is mission in what he says. Surely it is hardly credible he would have had to spend years of life in prison, and other years in exile or under house arrest, simply for criticizing remote peoples and their faiths or for advocating a return to traditional Islam. The reason he is seen as a revolutionary is that the line he draws between a religion of revolution and a religion of legitimation divides the social structure of Iran itself. When he inveighs against medieval Roman Catholic authorities, his real target is the Shah. He does not have to say this, for his Iranian listeners will understand.

This is the pathos of the speeches he delivers on two kinds of religion. Here is a man under severe political pressure, shortly to face years of prison, house arrest, and death. His words, however, are not about himself, but about drawing a line between the false and the true, and for that line he is willing to pledge his life.

Andrew Burgess
Albuquerque, NM
November 3, 1988

Endnotes to the Foreword

1. "A Descriptive Catalogue," *Poetry and Prose of William Blake,* ed. Geoffrey Keynes (London: Nonesuch Press, 1948), p. 617.

2. See "An Outline of Dr. Shariati's Life and Career," in *What is to be Done?* Edited and Annotated by Farhang Rajaee (Houston: Institute for Research and Islamic Studies, 1986), pp. xvii-xix.

3. See for example Camilo Torres, *Camilo Torres' Life and Message* (Springfield, Ill.: Templegate, 1968; Carlos Alberto Libanio Christo, *Against Principalities and Powers: Letters from a Brazilian Jail,* (Maryknoll: Orbis, 1975); Gustavo Gutierrez, *A Theology of Liberation,* (Maryknoll, New York: Orbis, 1973).

4. *A History of the Church in Latin America: Colonialism to Liberation, 1492-1979* (Grand Rapids, Mich.: Eerdmans, 1981).

5. The English translation of this book and the previous, *Hajj: Reflections on its Rituals* are to be published in the Spring of 1989 by ABJAD, Book Designers and Builders.

Introduction

Religion vs Religion consists of two lectures Ali Shariati gave at the Husayniyah Center in Tehran on August 12 and 13, 1970. In them he puts forth a most remarkable thesis, that throughout history, religion has fought against religion and not a non-religion as we have come to believe.

That is, monotheism, the religion of the belief that God is One, the religion brought by the Prophet Abraham which is called *din al-hanif*, 'the rightful religion', has continuously, throughout history, had to struggle against the religion of denying that there is One God or believing that there is no God (*kufr*, disbelief, infidelity, atheism) or against the religion of believing that there are multiple gods (*shirk*, polytheism, multitheism), the latter of which has branched into idolatry .

This is the first barrier to a correct understanding of religion and a distinction which he claims the European intellectual, in particular, Karl Marx, overlooked. He, along with European Christian intellectuals who had become critical of religion, had not understood the importance of this difference. They only observed religion as being practiced through what sociology of religions calls its 'priestly function' of celebrating the status quo, whatever it happened to be, without regard to its being in the right or in the wrong.

But religion throughout history has had another far more significant function, one which came through the divinely selected Prophets, that is, to call the people or nation they addressed into account. This 'prophetic function' of religion acted "as a vehicle of protest against accepted values and present policies of the dominant society".[1]

It is the significance of this function that was overlooked in the Renaissance, Reformation and Age of Enlightenment as Europeans reacted to the priestly misuse of religion assuming that religion was out to control people's minds, by holding the reigns of power and wealth, thereby exploiting and oppressing the human being in God's Name! God forbid!

The prophetic function is a two-dimensional confrontation. It confronts the 'self' and its 'psychological idols' within and/or 'socio-political idols' in the externalized world.

The confrontation in both cases arises through the two-fold awakening of consciousness of self and of society. Awareness needs to confront the self within and uncover the disguises without. Shariati and other Iranian Muslim activists, 'religious scholars' and 'intellectuals', alike, who had understood the prophetic function of religion developed this particular consciousness which manifested itself in an ability to 'discern things as they really are'. It is a prophetic-like power which Prophets like Abraham, Moses, Jesus and Muhammad, peace be upon them, had and a study of their methods teaches this ability. A person who has this ability is referred to in Islamic terms as an 'idol-destroyer'.

One has to begin on the psychological level with consciousness of self, become conscious of one's inward 'idols' before one has the ability to become conscious of them in the external world and in their socio-political guise. If one proceeds in the opposite direction, a credibility gap will develop as one tries to help others develop consciousness of these false gods before one has sorted them out inwardly. The reverse process does not produce authenticity and one readily falls into the 'priestly function' of religion, the very thing one found objection with in the first place when at the verge of self and social consciousness.

Psychological idols quite obviously do not mean statues, as Shariati explains. He writes in *Hajj: Reflections on its Rituals* [2] that it is that which one must 'destroy' of oneself for it is that which holds back one's full attachment to God. By 'destroy' he means become fully conscious of the power that 'it' has over you. He says:

Forms of Psychological Idols

"What is it? Your rank? Your reputation? Your position? Your profession? Your wealth? Your home? Your garden? Your automobile? Your beloved? Your family? Your knowledge? Your title? Your art? Your spirituality? Your dress? Your fame? Your sign? Your soul? Your youth? Your beauty?

"I do not know. You yourself know this....I can only give its signs to you: Whatever weakens you upon the way of faith. Whatever calls you to stop in your movement. Whatever brings doubt to your responsibility. Whatever is attached to you and holds you back. Whatever you have set your heart upon which does not allow you to hear the message in order to admit the Truth. Whatever causes you to flee. Whatever leads you towards justification, legitimation, and compromise-seeking hermeneutics and love which makes you blind and deaf."[3]

Idols at the Socio-political Level

The situation becomes more complicated at the socio-political level. When the forces of power, prestige or priesthood, right or wrong, directly confront the prophetic-function addressing it, in their own guise of denying the existence of God or legitimating their belief in the existence of gods, the confrontation is direct and straightforward: monotheism vs atheism (*kufr*); monotheism vs multitheism (*shirk*); monotheism vs. tyrannical ruler (*taghut*); monotheism vs. idolatry. This type has been recorded in history although not presented on its own terms. That is, emphasis is given to power and victory, however temporary it may be, rather than addressing the principles and human values involved.

The difficult situation to detect is one when the forces of *kufr* or the forces of multitheism put on the disguise of monotheists and pretend, with their words, to be what they are not in their hearts: monotheism vs hypocrisy (*nifaq*).

Outwardly expressing belief in the One God and support for this belief, they continuously undermine its progress and ultimate victory. It is Shariati's view, a view consistently to be found in all of his works, that it is these forces which have plagued Islamic history and brought it to the point which it now holds. These forces awakened to the fact that if they were to become indirect, they would have greater success in preventing the spread of God's religion, the implementation of which was the very cause of Creation. These forces went underground, changed their clothes and came out looking like people full of religious faith and emotion and only now and again in the 1400 years of Islamic history have conscious individuals been able to perform the prophetic-like function of religion, distinguishing between truth and falsehood and exposing the contradictions and hypocrisy.

Revelation Ended with the Seal but the Prophetic-like Function of Calling into Account Lives On

In the Islamic view, Muhammad, peace and the mercy of God be upon him and his household, was the Seal of Prophets. Revelation ended with him and there will be no Prophet until the end of time when the Prophet Jesus will return following the appearance of a savior.[4] But the function of prophethood, calling people and nations into account, did not end when revelation ended but was, rather, a responsibility given to all of humanity to continue. Few, however, have the courage to take up the gauntlet, to gain consciousness of their own inadequacies and work on them as they try to awaken others to the falseness of their human situation. This responsibility in Shariati's view is that of enlightened religious scholars and intellectuals.[5]

Multitheism and Society

Again we return to *Hajj: Reflections on its Rituals*: ".[6] And here it is a social system which is referred to, class infrastructure, people and powers ruling people, those who are involved in the destiny of people, people in their relation to God and to claimants of a deity. Here basic evil and the perpetual enemy of people are referred to, victims, not human kind or human society. Rather a class, 'people'.

"It is only in relation to people that an idol is built and a *taghut* is worshipped, can come to claim God's position, God's Qualities and the title and particularities of God. It is only in relation to God with the people not with the world and nature that it intervenes so that the servants of God are drawn to enslavement and despite the imagination of scholars who think in solitude - who read facts in textbooks not in the context of realities - *tawhid* and *shirk* are not just two philosophical views or theological ideas to be discussed within the four walls of schools and temples.

"Rather they are living realities, in the depths of the human being's primordial nature, in the context of the life of the masses, in the heart of encounters, contradictions, the movement of history, the class war of people and enemies of people throughout time. Opposed to what those thinkers who think in solitude imagine, *shirk* is a religion, a religion ruling over history. Yea, the opium of the people!

"And *tawhid*, the condemned religion of history. The blood of people. The primordial nature, mission, weapon of the people and the greatest and most profound, most clandestine tragedy of humanity - so much so that intellectuals have still not discovered it - is the enslavement of people with the sole claim of freedom of the people. The death and abjectness of the people with the capital resources of life and the honor of the people! How? By metamorphosizing religion through religion! The great hypocrisy of history. Iblis in the sacred image of God!"[7]

Multitheists Legitimate Religion

He goes on to give the legitimations of the false religion: "Have patience, my religious brother. Leave the world to those who are of it. Let hunger be the capital for the pardon of your sins. Forebear the hell of life for the rewards of paradise in the Hereafter. If you only knew the reward of people who tolerate oppression and poverty in this world! Keep your stomach empty of food, O brother, in order to see the light of wisdom in it. 'What is the remedy?' Whatever befalls us. The pen of destiny has written on our foreheads from before: The prosperous are prosperous from their mother's womb and the wretched are wretched from their mother's womb. Every protest is a protest against the Will of God. Give thanks for His giving or non-giving.'

" ' Let the deeds of everyone be accounted for on the Day of Reckoning. Be patient with oppression and give thanks for poverty. Do not breathe a word so that you do not lose the reward of the patient in the Hereafter. Release your body so as not to require clothes! Do not forget that the protest of a creature is protest against the Creator. The accounting of Truth and justice is the work of God, not the masses. In death, not in life. Do not pass judgement for the

Judge of the judgment is God. Do not be shamed on the Day of Resurrection when you see that God, the Merciful, the Compassionate forgives the oppressor who you had not forgiven in this world. Everyone is responsible for his own deeds." And so on and so on. The religion of multitheism continues to deceive people into believing that this is God's way.

He continues, "And it is because of this [these kinds of legitimations and justifications] that throughout history, wherever a Prophet was appointed by God from among the people themselves or a seeker of justice arose from among the people with the responsibility of calling the children of Abel - the people - to monotheism, justice and consciousness, they attacked him with full force and killed him. And then after a full generation or less, they would take on the role of mourners of him, heirs to his faith and custodians of his *ummah* . If a Prophet was victorious over them, they submitted themselves, changed their clothes and in a full generation or less became his Caliph and deputy, master of his banner, Book, seal and sword!....

"Moses drowns Pharaoh in the waters of the Nile with the miraculous power of the whitened hand of monotheism, buries Korah in the earth and effaces the religion of witchcraft with the staff of the mission. But Pharaoh drowned in the Nile immediately raises his head out of the River Jordan and becomes the heir of Moses in the name of Shamoon, takes the staff of Moses in hand instead of the whip. The sorcerers of Pharaoh become the sons of Aaron and companions of Moses, taking in hand the Pentateuch, instead of the magic staff. Balaam becomes the Sign of God. Korah receives the trust of the monotheistic people; and all three swallow up Palestine in the name of the Promised Land."

This continues throughout history and then, more recently, "The revolution in France uproots feudalism. Korah, the landlord, is stoned in the countryside. He immediately returns to town and becomes a banker. Pharaoh's head is cut by the blade of the guillotine of the revolution. He is stoned out of the palace of Versailles but with the treasure of Korah and the witchcraft of Balaam, he pops his head out of the democratic ballot box."....⁵

Shariati Warns of the Dangers of Multitheism

"Your enemy is not always armed or an army. It is not always eternal, not always apparent. Sometimes it is: a system; an emotion; a thought; a possession; a method of life; a method of work; a way of thinking; a tool of work; in the form of productivity; a kind of consumption; a culture; cultural colonialism; religious deception; class exploitation; the mass media. Sometimes it is bureaucracy, technocracy and automation; chauvinism, nationalism or racism; the egotism of Nazism, the gold diggers of the bourgeoisie or militarism's love of coercion. Sometimes it is the worship of pleasure, of epicurianism, of a subjective idealism or objective materialism...

"These are the idols of the new multitheism, the Lat and Uzza of the new Quraysh, three hundred and sixty idols, the Ka'bah of this civilization!

"Understanding the forms that multitheism takes, you realize what the worship of God is. How extensive is the meaning and greatness of the mission of monotheism!" [9]

Conclusion

Religion vs Religion, translated here for the first time in English, awakened religious and prophetic-like consciousness, bringing literally thousands of young people back to faith and belief in God. Shariati, in his inimitable way, clearly marks the lines and points out the signs that distinguish a divinely-imitative religion manifested throughout history in a 'priestly-function' of, right or wrong, celebrating a nation and a divinely-originated religion and its 'prophetic-function' of distinguishing between right and wrong and then calling a nation into account.

Laleh Bakhtiar
Albuquerque, NM
October 12, 1988

Endnotes to the Introduction
1. Patrick McNamara, *Religion: North American Style,* p. 31.
2. Translated and published by ABJAD, p. 135.
3. *Ibid.,* p. 137.
4. *Ibid.,* p. 138.
5. *Ibid.,* p. 139.
6. *Ibid.*
7. *Ibid.*
8. *Ibid.*
9. *Op. cit.,* p. 139.

Lecture One

Introduction
The subject I will discuss for these two nights - tonight and tomorrow night - just as announced, is religion* vs. religion. There may be an ambiguity in this phrase. The ambiguity is a consequence of the fact that we have, up until now, thought that religion was continuously opposed by disbelief, and that throughout history, the struggle has been between religion and non-religion. It is because of this that the interpretation of 'religion vs. religion' may seem foreign, ambiguous, strange and unacceptable.

Recently I have become attentive to the fact - perhaps I was aware of it some time ago but not with the same clarity and precision that I now sense - that opposed to this concept, throughout history, religion has always fought against religion and never in the sense that we understand today, religion against non-religion.

When history is spoken about, it is not the current usage of the word 'history', that is, 'the history of the appearance of civilization and writing', that I refer to. It is the beginning of the social life of the present day human being upon this earth. Thus, whereas the beginning of writing has a 6000 year old history, the history I am speaking about is more than 20,000 or 40,000 years old. That is, through various fields - archeology, history, geology, the study of myths and legends - we have more or less a summary knowledge of the first human being, his life- style, type of belief and the direction of social changes to the present time.

Throughout all of these ages, the first part of which has been told through myths and legends, as we grow close to today, it becomes more clear and better documented and history itself begins to tell us that continuously, in all stages, religion has stood up against religion and that throughout history, without exception, it has been religion which has, in unbroken succession, fought against religion. Why? Because history knows no era or society which lacks religion. That is, there is no historical precedence of a non-religious society. There has been no non-religious human being in any race, in any era, in any phase of social change on any part of the earth.

In more recent years, from the age when civilization, thought, reasoning and philosophy began to grow, we occasionally encounter individuals who did not accept the Resurrection or God, but never throughout history have these individuals taken the form of a class, a group or a society.

According to Alexis Carrel,* past history has continuously consisted of societies and these societies were, in a general sense, religiously structured. The pivot, heart and basis of every society was a deity, a religious faith, a prophet or a religious book and even the physical form of every city was a sign of the spiritual condition of the society.

Throughout the Middle Ages and even before Jesus, peace be upon him, in the East and in the West, all of the cities consisted of a complex of houses or a complex of buildings - where these buildings were often tribal - but in every phase of a tribe, based upon aristocracy or based upon its social condition, it was placed in the high point, greater, more important and closer to the heart of the city or else in the form of classlessness. At any rate, that which existed in all of the large cities,   which is similar in all civilizations of the East and the West, is this that all of these cities were symbolic. A symbolic city is a city which shows itself in a clear and determined form.

This symbol, which is a sign of the character of the great city, was a temple whereas this sign today is clearly losing its role. For instance, Tehran is not a symbolic city. That is, if we look at the collection of building positions, we see that they have not been joined around an axis, a building, a religious structure or even a non-religious one in the sense that the buildings do not have a heart or an axis. But in an aerial photograph of the city of Mashhad, it is clear that this city is symbolic, that it is a city whose complex of buildings have been joined around an axis which is the heart and the sponsor of the city.

Why were these cities symbolic? Because, essentially, no architecture - whether it be the architecture of a civilization, of a nation or of a city - existed without a religious explanation. All of the books that we can look at, even in our own Persian language, books which have been written about cities like *The History of Qum, Balkh, Bukhara, Nishabur, The Virtues of Balkh,* etc. which describe cities, all of them begin with a religious story. That is, they could not convince themselves that such a large city would be built and would appear because of a factor other than a religious factor or that they be built for a reason other than a religious and spiritual one. It was always that a prophet had been buried there or that it was built upon the basis of a religious miracle or that later it would be that something sacred or a religious person, was to be buried there. At any rate, the legitimation in every case is a religious legitimation.

This shows that, in general, all ancient societies, whether they were in the form of classes or classlessness or tribal or tribalessness, whether they took the form of a great empire like that of Rome or that of separate city-states like those of Greece, whether in the form of tribes like the Arabs, whether they were civilized and developed or backward and degenerated, in all races, human gatherings have a single spirit, called a religious spirit and ancient man, in every era and of whatever thought, is a religious human being. Thus the phrase, 'non- religious' which today we understand from the word 'disbelief' (*kufr*)* did not exist in the sense of atheism*, a lack of belief in the metaphysical, in the Resurrection, in the Unseen, in God, in the sacred or the existence of One or several gods in the world, because all people held these principles in common.

That which today we define as atheism, non-religion or anti-religion, is a very new concept. That is, it relates to the last two or three centuries. It refers to that which took place after the Middle Ages. It is a definition which has been imported into the East in the form of a western intellectual product, that *kufr* means a lack of belief of a human being in God, in the metaphysical and in another world. In Islam, in all ancient texts, in all histories, in all religions, when *kufr* is spoken about, it is not in the sense of non-religion. Why? Because there was so such thing as non-religion.

Thus, *kufr* (as defined today as disbelief, infidelity* or unbelief) was itself a religion like a religion which refers to another religion as *kufr*, just as the other religion of *kufr* refers to yet other faiths as being among those who are *kufr*. *Kufr*, then, means another religion, not a non-religion.

Thus, throughout history, whether it be the history of the Abrahamic religions or the religions of the East or the West - in whatever form it takes - wherever a prophet or a religious revolution appeared in the name of religion, it was first manifested in spite of and in opposition to the existing religion of its own age and secondly, the first group or force which arose against this religion, stood against it, persevered and brought about a struggle, was religion.

Here we encounter an extremely important point which solves the most basic problem of the judgment today of intellectuals of the world and also we can, then, test and scientifically and historically analyze the greatest judgment which all of the intellectuals of the world have made in relation to religion.

This judgment - that is, the judgment of intellectuals in relation to religion - that religion opposes civilization, progress, people and liberty or that it is inattentive to them - is a judgment which came into being based upon objective and precise scholarly studies of the realities and continuous historical experiences. It is not a curse. It is not an expression of fantasy that is born of vengeance and hatred or evil intentions and malice. Rather, it rests upon experience and is an accurate scholarly conclusion based upon realities existing in history, in human societies and in the life of the human being.

But why, at the same time, in my opinion, is the judgment not correct? Because even we who are followers of a religion, that is, we who are religious types, do not know that, throughout history, there have been two religions - in different forms but, in reality, one - which quarreled, were at war and in conflict with one another. Not only do these two religions have differences with one another, but, as I said, essentially an ideological and religious war in the past was a war between these two religions but for a special reason, we are not aware of it at the present time.

Thus, as a result, first of all, we have a general opinion about religion. We prove it in a general way and then prove it in our own religion in a particular way. But this method is wrong. It is a mistake which the anti-religious forces in the last two or three centuries have made, in particular, in the 19th century, which is the peak of objection to religion in Europe, for they were not able to separate these two religions from each other whereas these two religions not only have no resemblance to each other, but they are even hostile and contradictory to one another and, essentially, they continuously, without any interruption, throughout history, fought with each other, still do and will continue to do so.

Their judgment related to one line of this religion and was correct and experienced, based upon historical realities, but they were unaware of the line opposite this religion - which was itself a religion - just as we who are religious are unaware of the other. This correct judgment of theirs which conforms to half of the realities was automatically made into a generalization to include all of the realities, i.e. even the other contradictory half, that is, the contradictory line to this religion and the mistake lies here.

Just as I said, these two religions, in their various forms, differ from one another. If we want to weigh all of the qualities of these two religions and count their qualities, whatever quality we prove in one way for one of them, we are obliged to negate that very same quality for the other religion.

As the terms I use are terms which we are all familiar with, but as they have another meaning, I ask that as soon as I use a term, you not define it according to the meaning which you previously had in mind. Rather, define and judge the word in vogue according to the special definition which I use.

Let me first give a word of explanation of the ambiguity which exists in these words and which is in vogue, causing mingling of these two subjects which are completely separate. They are: *kufr, shirk** (multitheism)* and paganism* or idolatry* which we continuously use in religious terminology.

Kufr(Denying the Truth)
Kufr means to cover or to plant, i.e. where in farming, a seed is planted and then covered over with earth. In the hearts of

people, a truth exists but because for certain reasons, the truth is covered over by a curtain of ignorance, malice, self-seeking interests or absolute foolishness, it is called *kufr*. This *kufr*, however, does not mean the covering over the truth of religion by means of a non-religion. Rather, it means covering over the truth of religion by means of another religion.

Multitheism *(Shirk)*＊

Shirk or multitheism does not mean godlessness. Rather, multitheists have more gods than we do! A multitheist is not a person who does not believe in a deity. It is not a person who does not worship a deity. As we know, those who opposed Jesus, Moses and Abraham are multitheists, not godless people.

Who are multitheists? They are not people who do not believe in a deity. They are people who believe in more than there is. That is, they have extra gods. They are worshippers of excessive deities. Thus, from the scholarly point of view, a person who does not have a religious belief and religious sensibilities cannot be called a multitheist because multitheists have deities.

They have various deities. They believe in their servitude in relation to these deities and in the influence of these deities in the destiny of the world and their own fate. Thus, just as we look at God, a multitheist looks at his own gods.

Therefore, from the point of view of emotions, a multitheist is religious. He or she is a religious individual but from the point of view of meaning and from the point of view of religious realities, he or she is a person who has gone astray. A religion which has gone astray is something other than a non-religion. Thus, multitheism is a religion and it is known by some as the oldest form of religion among human societies.

Idolism

Idolism is a special form of the religion of multitheism. It is not synonymous with it. Multitheism has been recognized as being a religion of the common people throughout history and, in one phase, it became manifested in the form of idolism. Thus, idolism means the making of statues or sacred things which, from the point of view of its followers, that is, the followers of the religion of multitheism, are sacred or belong to the sacred.

That is, they are either similar to a god or they believe that basically it is a god or they believe that they are intermediaries or the representatives of a god and, at any rate, they believe that each of these gods is effective in a part of the workings of life and the world. Thus, idolism refers to one of the factions of the religion of multitheism.

In the Holy Quran, when they (multitheists, idolaters) are attacked or when discussions are held with them and criticism is made of them, attempts are made so that dialogues be held in more general terms with them and include both multitheists and idolaters. Why? So that later this very judgment which has presently come to mind, not come into being and we not imagine that the Islamic movement only opposes those existing forms of idolism but rather, understand that the attack of Islam, following the monotheistic movements of the past, is an attack on the roots of the religion of multitheism in a general way and in whatever form it took, including the form of the worship of statues and we imagine that we should only recognize the opposition (that is, the religion of multitheism) when it takes the form of idolism, for the Holy Quran says, *"Do you worship things which you (yourselves) carve?"* (37:95)

Has it only been statues of wood and stone which we constructed with our hands throughout history and throughout the width and breadth of geographic lands that we then worshipped? No. Multitheism was and is manifested in hundreds of physical and non-physical forms as one of the common religions in the history of humanity. One of the its forms, at the present time, in all human societies, is that of idolism in the form of African or Arabian ignorance.

This, *"Do you worship those things which you (yourselves) carve?"* is a general principle. It is a description of the manner of religious worship in the religion of multitheism. This religion of multitheism moved forward, throughout history, side by side and step by step, exactly parallel with the religion of monotheism and it continues to move forward with it. It never ended with the story of Abraham or with the manifestation of Islam. Rather, it still continues.

Monotheism (*tawhid*)*

This is a discussion which relates to the history of religions but I will endeavor to speak in our own terms of Islam and speak from our culture. In a religious front, that is, in one of these two fronts, there is the worship of the One God, God in the Name of the Awake, Willed, Creator and Determiner of the universe. These are Qualities of God in all the Abrahamic religions. There is the Quality of Creator, that is, He created all of the world. There is the Quality of the Divine Will, that is, the world moves and is guided through His Will.

Another Quality is that which rules over existence and which has Vision and Absolute Awareness of all of the universe. At the same time, God is the direction towards which existence and creation moves and He determines the goal of the universe.

The worship of this Absolute Power which is the great call of all of the Abrahamic Traditions, essentially, the goal of Abraham in announcing this well-known cry, consisted of the invitation to all human beings to worship the One Power in existence, to orient their attention to one direction in creation, to believe in one effective power in all of existence and one place of refuge throughout life.

This invitation, which in history is announced as being the invitation to monotheism, *tawhid*, has a material and this-worldly side, as well. It is clear when a group believes that all of this creation is built by one Power and that all of this created world, whether human or animal, whether plant or even inanimate, one Force rules and that other than He, there is no effect and that all things, forms, colors, types and substances, are built by the One Creator, this world view of Divine Unity and the Unity of God in Existence, logically and intellectually requires the unity of humanity upon the earth.

That is, when monotheism announces that all of creation is one empire, in the hands of one Power and that all human beings are one Source, are guided through one Will, are oriented towards one way, are made of one type, have One God, and that all powers, symbols, manifestations, values and signs must be destroyed before Him, when a person like myself, who believes in monotheism, looks at the world, I automatically see this world as having a total, living form. I see a Universal, a Spirit, a Power which rules over this physical form. Thus it is a universal. Also, when I look at all of humanity, as a unified genus, I look at it with one value because it has been created by one Hand and there is one Order.

This religion of monotheism, one of the two religions, is based upon the worship of One God, the belief in one Power for all of Creation and all of the fate of humanity in history. As I have said, the unity of God, of necessity, brings about the unity of the universe and the unity of the human being.

On the other hand, this particular belief of humanity is the primordial desire of human beings for the worship of one Power, the belief in one Sanctity (as Durkheim* says) or the belief in the unseen (as the Holy Quran says). This belief is part of the primordial nature, *fitrat* * of humanity which has continuously existed. A sign of something being *fitri** is first, its lasting quality and, then, its presence in all areas and all places. Thus these signs show that something is *fitri*.

If we follow a nation throughout its history, we see worship has endured. If we look at the world in any one era, we see it has always existed in all places and this shows that worship is instinctive, based in one's primordial nature.

This feeling of worship brought by the religion of monotheism brings about the recognition of the Power which encompasses the world and, as a result, ends in the recognition of the living world in its powerful, sensitive form which contains a Will and a goal. This desire, by means of the religion of monotheism, is also manifested in history in the form of a belief in the unity of humanity, the unity of all races, all classes, all families and all individuals, the unity of rights and the unity of honor.

Preventing the Spread of Monotheism

This very religious feeling, on the other hand, finds continuance in the history of religions, in the form of multitheism. The continuation takes a form in every era which brings into being the greatest power to confront the first religion which we mentioned. It brings into being the greatest power to resist and to prevent the spread of the religion of monotheism.

There is not sufficient time for me to describe all religions from this point of view but with the familiarity and knowledge that we have, at least about the great prophets. Look at Moses in the Pentateuch*, in stories relating to it and books on it and Pentateuchial culture and even in the Quran and Islamic Traditions: the greatest forces which confronted Moses and, more than anything else, harmed Moses' movement have been shown to be first, the Samaritan and the second, Balaam.

The Samaritan*
After a great deal of anguish and struggle and even after his victory of making the One God familiar to his people in his society, Moses destroys calf worship and idolism which was one of the types of multitheism in those days. After all this, the Samaritan once again builds a calf. He takes advantage of the slightest opportunity, which was the absence of Moses, so that the people worship the calf.

This person who built the calf so that people worship it instead of Yahweh, God, Allah, was not a godless or non-religious person. He was a believer in religion. He was a preacher and even a religious leader.

Balaam*
Is he a materialist philosopher? Is he a temporalist? Is he a Metternich or a Schopenhauer? No. Balaam is the greatest priest of that time.   The religion of the people turned around this individual and it is because of this that he arises, in spite of Moses, and confront's Moses' movement. As the religion, emotions and faith of the people were in his hands, he could undertake the greatest struggle in history to confront the truth - the religion of monotheism - and strike the most effective blows.

The Pharisees*
Let us look at Jesus. His sermons, his sufferings and the blows which Jesus withstood until close to the end of his life, which terminates in his crucifixion, according to Judeo-Christian traditions, when he is destroyed, when he is defeated, when he bears all of the blows and treason, all of the pressures, all of the slander, all of the evil words and the ugliest of insults which are given in relation to him and his mother, all were done at the hands of the Pharisees.

Who were the Pharisees? The Pharisees were the defenders and masters of the religion of the time. They were not materialists. They were not atheists. They were not temporalists. There were no materialists at that time. Those who confronted Jesus and his followers were believers, pursuers and preachers of the religion of multitheism.

Let us look at the Prophet of Islam. Were the several people who stood before him at the battles of Uhud,* at Ta'if,* at Badr,* at Makkah, with swords unsheathed, godless men? Were they essentially not believers lacking in religious feelings? Not one person can be found who was not. Not even one. All were people who either in truth or hypocritically believed.

The reason they gave as their battle cry was that the Prophet, the son of Abd Allah* and his followers must be done away with, "because they want to destroy the honor and respect of Abraham's house". Why? "Because they reject our principles, sacredness and beliefs. Because they want to destroy this house and this sacred land of Makkah. Because they want to break our sacredness, our idols, our temples and our priests who stand behind us and the gods." Thus, the battle cry of the Quraysh*, the battle cry of all of the Arabs who fought against Islam, throughout the lifetime of the Prophet, was the cry of 'religion vs. religion'.

After the Prophet of Islam, this very same battle cry begins in another form. Had disbelief arisen and stood before Ali, before the movement which continued the spirit of Islam, which wanted to continue it? Was it godlessness and non-religion? Or the reasoning that God does not exist? Or was it the belief in a religion which brought about the war between the Umayyid* tribe and the followers of Ali,* the war between the descendants of Abbas* and the family of the Prophet in opposition to this religion?

The Paradox

Among the particularities of that religion, that is, the Abrahamic religion - we refer to it as the Abrahamic religion because everyone more readily understand this - the monotheistic religion, is the worship of God. Throughout history, one religion and one creed was announced before all of these movements of multitheism. According to our belief and according to the philosophy of history, from Adam to the Seal* (the Prophet of Islam), and continuously until the end of the history of humanity, the worship of One Deity, as the Creator of the world, was announced, Who Determines all of the values of human beings and the goal of history in the life of humanity.

This was announced to stand before the worship of the arrogant ruler who rebels against God's Commands, the *taghut** to stand before this movement which invited humanity to submit before this great Beloved of Existence, this great secret of Creation, this great goal of Creation which ended and terminated in God. It was announced to submit before this System and before this goal. Confronting this goal, which is called Islam, and, as Islam itself describes it, 'submission' (*islam*) is the name of all true religions, were those who worshipped an arrogant leader who rebelled against God's commands ('*ibadu taghut*).

But this religion of monotheism, while it invites humanity to submit before God, in the same way and for this very reason, it invites humanity to rebel against anything that is other than He. opposed to this, the religion of multitheism or *shirk* invites humanity to rebel against this great Beloved of Existence, before this invitation of Islam to God, Who is the meaning of all of existence and the eternal goal of all life, and to rebel against the religion of Islam and it calls this 'surrender'. It terminates automatically in surrender and slavery to hundreds of other powers, to hundreds of other polarizations and forces, where each pole, each power, each class and each group has a god.

Multitheism means servitude. It means rebelling against servitude to God and, at the same time, it means surrender, disgrace and the enslavement of humanity in bondage to the idols, that is, that which deceivers, liars, ignorance and oppression all built with the help of one another is to invite people to servitude and worship of other than God.

This is rebellion against God's commands, rebellion before the great Power of Being and surrender to, "*that which you (yourselves) carved,*" no matter what it wants to be, whether it be Lat* or Uzza* or a machine or virtues or capital, whether blood or ancestor, whatever it is in any period, these are idols before Allah, before God.

Among the particularities of the monotheistic religion is its position of attack and revolution. Among the particularities of the religion of multitheism, in its general sense, is the legitimation of the status quo.

What does a revolutionary religion mean?

A revolutionary religion gives an individual, that is, an individual who believes in it, who is trained in the school of thought or *maktab** of this religion, the ability to criticize life in all its material, spiritual and social aspects. It gives the mission and duty to destroy, to change and to eliminate that which one does not accept and believes to be invalid and replace it with that which one knows and recognizes as being the truth.

The particularity of the religion of monotheism is that it does not show indifference before it. Look at all of the prophets. It clearly shows that these monotheistic religions, in their first state at the beginning of their manifestation, which is the height of their purity and their lucidity, and they have not changed in the least bit, nor have they been transformed, take the form of a movement against the status quo, take the form of rebellion against defilement and oppression, a rebellion which announces servitude to the creator, that is, the cause of creation and submission to the Laws of Existence, which are the manifestation of the Laws of God.

Look at all religions. Look at Moses. Did Moses not rebel before three symbols? Korah*, the greatest capitalist of his time. Balaam, the greatest priest of that deviated religion of multitheism. And the Pharaoh, the greatest symbol of political power of his time. Did he not arise against the status quo?

What was the status quo? Enslavement and humiliation by the minority of the Sebtians towards another race called the Coptics. Moses' movement was a struggle against racial discrimination which was the superiority of the Coptics over the Sebtians, a struggle against the social situation, which was the domination of one race over another race, or the enslavement of a race. It is to replace an ideal. It is the realization of a clear purpose for life and society which is the salvation of an enslaved race, its guidance and its migration to the promised land. It is the development of a society based upon an ideology and based upon a social school in which an arrogant leader who rebels against God's Command, who is the legitimizer of discrimination, is destroyed and replaced by monotheism which signifies the unity of society and humanity.

What does a religion of legitimation mean?

The endeavors of the religion of multitheism or *shirk* are always to legitimate and defend the status quo by making use of metaphysical beliefs, a belief in god or gods, a belief in the Resurrection, that is, legitimating the belief in the Resurrection, and distorting the belief in unseen powers and distorting all principles of religious beliefs.

That is, in the name of religion, people are made to believe, "The situation which you have or which your society has is a situation which you and your society must have because this is the manifestation of God's Will. It is destiny and fate."

Destiny or fate, in the sense that we understand it today is a souvenir concocted by Mu'awiyah.* History clearly shows that belief in a fate or pre-determination was brought into being by the Umayyids. Because of their belief in pre-determination, Muslims were held back from taking any kind of responsibility or action or making criticism. Pre-determination means accepting that which is and whatever will happen.

Commanding to Good and Preventing Evil*

But see the Companions of the Holy Prophet who believe in their social responsibility at every moment, commanding to good or virtue and preventing evil or vice which exists in an absurd way in our minds and which cannot even be mentioned in an intellectual community, is that very thing which the intellectuals of Europe today have replaced with terms like 'human responsibility', 'artist's responsibility' and 'intellectual's responsibility'.

What does that which philosophy, art and literature speak about in terms of responsibility in today's society mean? It means exactly what commanding to good and preventing evil means but we have so made commanding to good and preventing evil that we actually command to good and prevent evil in a way whereby we repudiate it.

The Continuation of Multitheism

The religion of multitheism continued, throughout history, in two forms. As I said, the mission and goal of the religion of multitheism is to legitimate the status quo. What does the status quo mean?

We see that, throughout history, human societies are divided into the noble and unnoble, master and slave, abased and enslaving, ruler and ruled, captive and free, a group which has an essence, roots, race and is of a golden extraction and another group which lacks these. A nation which is more virtuous than another nation. A class which is continuously superior and has preference over another class.

This discrimination which the preferred and aristocratic group have always had from the beginning over other families, this 'multitheistic' belief which existed in life and its agent was also the prosperity of one group and the abasement of another group, was automatically to legitimate the situation which is exactly opposite 'monotheistic' belief which is the destroyer of this situation. The religion of multitheism says, "Multiple gods must come into being for the multiple realms and the multiple rules in the world so that multiple groups, multiple classes, multiple families, multiple races and multiple colors be realized in society upon the earth and continue."

One group can, with coercion, abase another group and then that coercive group itself takes the legal, social and economic rights of society but they are difficult to maintain and keep. This is why coercive forces, throughout history, always took hold of these resources and abased the majority but it has not been able to maintain its domination with coercion.

It is here that religion, that is, the religion of multitheism takes up the mission of preserving this situation. Its work was to make people submit, be content with the belief that whatever took place was God's Will, convince themselves that, "I am connected to a low class not only because my essence is lowly but because my god, my lord, my creator and my master are lower than the masters of other races, lower than the idols of that race, lower than the gods of the other race."

Thus, when this situation is like this, when the discrimination of race and class, which take the form of this religion of multitheism, are strengthened and firmed up, the status quo is always and forever supposed to be like this and it will continue in this way. This is why, throughout history, the class of developers and guardians of the religion of multitheism is always the highest class and has even more power, is more established and more wealthy than even the ruling class.

Look at the Sassanian era. The priests dominated over the princes and the military. Look at the Magis.* Look at the priests in Europe. Look at rabbis of the Israeli tribes and types like Balaam. Look at tribes, idolatrous tribes. Look at Africa and Australia, the religion of witch doctors, those who spoke of the unseen, the astrologers, those who claimed to be the preservers of the existing religion. They all held hands and moved alongside with the rulers or else they dominated over them. In Europe, sometimes more than 70% of the land was at the disposal of the priests. In the Sassanian era, more land was in the hands of the priests than any other landowners, that is, the feudalists or endowed for temples and Zoroastrian places of worship.

We see that the prophets, the prophets that we believe in and follow, as opposed to that which we think and imagine, these prophets stood before a religion which, throughout history, has legitimated the oppressive and inhuman situation of the life of ancient societies from the economic, ethical as well as intellectual point of view and the worship of arrogant rulers who rebelled against God's Commands, in a general sense and idolism, in a particular sense. It was these prophets who opposed the spread of multitheism.

The Roots of the Religion of Multitheism
Ownership of a Minority over an Abased Majority
The roots of this religion, the religion of multitheism, are economic. Its roots are in the ownership of a minority over the abased majority. It is this very factor of economics and the seeking of superiority which requires a religion in order to preserve and legitimate itself and eternalize its way of life. What factor is stronger than this religion that an individual automatically accept and be content with his abjectness.

Legimitation of the Status Quo
It has been this religion - the religion of multitheism which has continuously legitimated the status quo. In what form? One was the form of the belief in and accept the idea that the existence of several nations and the existence of several families were the effects of

God's Will. "It is metaphysical!"

Promotion of Class Superiority
So that they themselves, in opposition to the other class, would prosper through the privileges which were continuously, throughout the history of rulers, in the exclusive control of rulers and they always monopolized history.

Narcosis or Inner Surrender
Just as the anti-religious forces of today correctly say, the elements of the religion of multitheism consisted of ignorance, fear, discrimination, ownership and the preference of one class over another. These people, that is, those who are anti-religious, are correct. It is right that, "Religion is the opium of the masses of the people, " so that the people surrender to their abjectness, difficulties, wretchedness and ignorance, surrender to the static situation which they are obliged to have, surrender to the disgraceful fate which they and their ancestors were obliged to have and still have - an inner, ideological surrender.

Withholding Responsibility
Look at the Murji'ites*. The Murji'ites in Islamic society negate the responsibilities of every criminal in history. The Murji'ites say, "Why does God speak about the scales on the Day of Judgment? Because He will see to Mu'awiyah and Ali's accounts?" That is, "When He is the judge, then you should not speak. What's it to you who is in the right and who is in the wrong. You carry on with your life."

The Movement of Multitheism: Manifest and Hidden
The religion of multitheism moves in two forms in history. The first form is that of a straight path which we see in the history of religions, that is, the religion of the worship of beads, the worship of something which is taboo, the worship of Magi, the worship of new lords, the worship of several gods and the worship of spirits. This is the hierarchy of the religion of multitheism in the history of religions but these are the obvious forms of the religion of multitheism.
The second form is the hidden form of the religion of multithe-

ism which is more dangerous than any of the others and more noxious. It is this hidden form of the religion of multitheism which has caused more harm and done more damage to humanity and to the truth than anything else. That is, multitheism hides behind the mask of monotheism.

As soon as the prophets of monotheism arose and confronted multitheism, multitheism stood against them. If these prophets were victorious and they were able to make multitheism fall to its knees, then multitheism would continue in its hidden form through the followers, successors and those who continued its way in the shape of monotheism.

This is why we see that when Balaam, who stood before Moses, is removed from the way as a result of the movement of Moses, he takes the form of the rabbi of the religion of Moses and the form of the Pharisees who murdered Jesus.[*]

It is this group which destroys Jesus and stands alongside the idolatrous Caesar of Rome against the defenders of monotheism. They work together and play out their roles together. They are either followers of that very group which stood against Moses or they are followers of that group which fled with Moses. They are the same Balaam and the Samaritan who now appear dressed in the clothes of the religion of Moses.

The priests of the Middle Ages committed more crimes than any criminal in the name of a religion which had historically been founded upon love, friendship, loyalty, patience, forgiveness and kindness in the name of Jesus, a person who was the theophany of peace and forgiveness - crimes the Mongols never even dreamed of and they shed more blood than any other criminals have ever done.

Are they, then, followers of the way of Jesus? Are they disciples of Jesus? Or are they continuing the way of the religion of multitheism? It is these very Pharisees who have now taken the form of priests so that they can turn Jesus' religion, from within, towards multitheism and they ended up doing so.

Thus, these words, spoken in the 19th century to the effect that "religion is the opium of the people," or "religion is so that people will patiently bear their abasement and wretchedness in this world in the name of hope after death", are correct. It is the opium of the people so that people find belief in the idea that whatever happens is in God's hands. It is because of God's Will and any efforts to try and change the situation, to try to improve the life of the people is to oppose God's Will. This is correct.

It is correct when the 18th and 19th centuries' scholars said, "Religion is born of the ignorance people have about scientific causes." And the fact that they said, "Religion is born of the delusive fear of people," and that, "Religion was born from discrimination, ownership and the abasement of the feudal age," is correct.

But which religion are they referring to? That very religion which always had history in its realm - other than the few moments which glowed like the splendor of lightening and they were extinguished - is that very religion of multitheism. Whether this religion of multitheism be in the name of the religion of monotheism, the religion of Moses or the religion of Jesus, or in the names of the Prophet's caliphs* or the Abbasid caliphate, all are in the name of the religion of monotheism, in the name of *jihad** and the Quran and the followers of the religion of multitheism even place the Holy Quran on the point of their spears.

The person who placed the Holy Quran on spearpoints was not a Quraysh who stood before the Prophet in support of Lat and Uzza. He could not preserve multitheism in this form. He enters from the inside and then places the holy Quran on the tip of his spear and strikes a blow at Ali. He strikes a blow at God's religion and the Prophet. In the name of the religion of Islam, once again, the religion of multitheism rules over history in the name of the caliphate of God's Messenger and in the name of a rule whose Constitution is the Holy Quran. Essentially, the caliph who goes upon the *jihad* and goes to the hajj, once again rules in the name of the religion of multitheism.

The religion of multitheism rules in the Middle Ages in the name of Jesus and in the name of Moses. They are among the founders of the monotheistic religion and once again, the religion of multitheism, rules in their name, the religion of legitimation, the religion of narcosis, the religion of statics and immobility, the religion of limitations, the religion which is indifferent to the life situation of people which always dominated over human societies throughout history. Those who said religion is born of fear, born of narcosis, is limiting, is born of the feudal age, spoke the truth because their reasoning is based upon history and historiography.

But they have not understood religion because they do not know religion or history. Whoever studies history will see that, throughout history, the work of religion has been just this - to preserve the religion of multitheism, either through assuming the name of monotheism or directly in the name of multitheism.

I have compared all of the names and qualities which refer to gods or a deity in the Abrahamic religions as well as the multitheist religions and I have seen that it is true that the religion of multitheism is born of the ignorance and fear of the people. Why?

Because religious multitheists, that is, people who propagate the religion of multitheism, are afraid of the people awakening, becoming literate, becoming scholars. They want knowledge to always be in the monopoly of one thing - themselves. Why?

Because as knowledge progresses, the religion of multitheism is destroyed for that which preserves the religion of multitheism is ignorance. The awakening of the people means the awakening of a spirit of objection and criticism in people, the divine ideal in people, the seeking of justice in people. This weakens and shakes the foundation of multitheism. Why?

Because throughout history that religion was the preserve and guardian of the status quo and this situation has existed throughout the history of humanity, from before the age of feudalism until the age of feudalism and afterwards in the East and in the West.

The same names of gods are continuously defined in the hierarchy of the multitheistic religions, that is, qualities or names like awe, dread and coercion in their particular despotic sense.

But all of the Names and Qualities of God in the Abrahamic Traditions reflect two ideas. That is, all the Names and Qualities which exist in the Abrahamic religions show two concepts: first, love and beauty and the worship of One Majesty and Beauty and second, that God is the refuge for the deprived and oppressed, the Master, the Lord and the One we rely upon.

Thus, we see that it is true that religions which existed in history and ruled, are born of ignorance and are born of the fear of the people from natural forces or powers whereas the Abrahamic religions, born of love, born of the need of a human being for a goal, the need for a single rule over the universe, for one direction or orientation in Creation, answer the need of the human being for the worship of Absolute Beauty and Absolute Perfection.

The prophets of this religion - the Abrahamic religions - continuously challenge all of the visages which rule, whether they be social or spiritual and all idols, whether they be logical, physical or human, whether they be economic or material. They challenge all of the manifestations of the religion of multitheism, that is, the religion of the status quo. Their responsibility and that of their followers was to uproot the status quo and replace it with justice. Justice, the scales and equity, which are continuously repeated in the Holy Quran, along with the Message of the Messenger, are in order to establish justice and equity and not in order to accept the status quo.

Conclusion

Thus, the conclusion that I want to make is that, throughout history, religion has not been confronted by non-religion. Religion has been confronted by religion. Religion has always fought with religion. The religion of monotheism, which is based upon awareness, consciousness, insight, love and the need of a person, a primordial, philosophical need, stands before the religion which is born of ignorance and fear.

Whenever a prophet was sent to the religion of monotheism, which is a revolutionary religion, to stand and confront the multitheistic religion, human beings were invited to follow the laws of nature which rule the universe in the universal, revolutionary journey of creation which is the theophany of the Divine Will. Essentially, the necessity of the religion of monotheism is rebellion, denial and saying 'no' before any other power.

And reciprocally, confronting the worship of God, there is the worship of an arrogant leader who rebels against God's Commands, a *taghut* who invited human beings to rebel before the system of truth which rules over the universe and the lives of humanity, resulting in the enslavement to the various idols which were representatives of multiple powers of society.

God and the deprived people form one front in the Pentateuch and the Gospels (those parts which have not been distorted and thus, deduction from them is possible), in the Holy Quran and everywhere without exception. Who opposes this front? The worshippers of an arrogant leader who rebels against the Commands of God, the *taghuti*. Who are they?

These very people, that is, those people who, according to the Holy Quran, are wealthy aristocrats, *mala'* ,* and insatiable people who live in ease and luxury, *mutrif*,* people who have ruled in their own society without having any responsibilities. Throughout history, the religion of the wealthy aristocrats and the insatiable people who live in ease and luxury ruled. It either ruled in a very clear and apparent way in its own name or it preserved itself under the cover of the religion of God and the people.

The religion of monotheism is a religion whose rule in history was not realized. In my opinion, this is one of the honors of Shi'ism that it did not accept that which was offered to the world in the Middle Ages as Islamic power. Its *jihad* was against the greedy eyes of imperialism and it saw the rule of the Caesars, not the caliphate of God's Prophet.

Thus, the Abrahamic religions or the monotheistic religion is that religion which continuously arose against the worship of an arrogant ruler who rebels against God's Commands, against the wealthy aristocrats and the insatiable people who live in ease and luxury and they invited people to arise against them.

The religion of monotheism announced that God is the supporter of the deprived and oppressed people. It addressed the people. Its goal has been the establishment of justice. The religion of monotheism is born of awareness, consciousness and the need for love, worship and the most extensive consciousness possible of the people but not as it has been realized in history. Rather, it took the form of a movement of criticism against history and it has never been realized in a perfect form.

At the same time, the religion of multitheism, the worship of an arrogant leader who rebels against God's commands, the wealthy aristocrats and the insatiable people who live in ease and luxury, that is, idolism, that is, the religion which legitimates the status quo and the religion of narcosis in history, continuously existed, held power and dominated.

I say to those intellectuals who always ask, "Why do you, an intellectual, rely so much on religion?" If I speak about religion, I do not speak about a religion which had been realized in the past and which ruled society. Rather, I speak about a religion whose goals are to do away with a religion which ruled over society throughout history. I speak about a religion the prophets of which arose to destroy the various forms which the religion of multitheism had taken and which at no time in history was realized by the religion of monotheism in a complete form from the point of view of society and the social life of the people.

Our responsibility is to put forth efforts for the realization of that religion in the future. This is the responsibility of humanity, so that in the future, the religion of monotheism, as it was announced through the prophets of monotheism in human society, replace the religions which render one senseless, narcotize and legitimate multitheism. Thus, my reliance upon religion is not a return to the past but rather the continuation of the way of history.

Lecture Two

Introduction

In the first part, I expressed what I meant by the phrase 'religion vs. religion'. As opposed to that which we may think, I recently realized (even though this discovery is not a very complicated philosophical or scientific one, but often very simple issues bring about very harmful results because we do not attend to them), religion has not, throughout history, fought against disbelief in the sense of what we feel it means, that is, non-religion - lack of religious belief - because in the past there was no society or class which was godless and without a religion. Throughout history, as history bears witness and all historic-sociological documents show, religious sociology and all historical research of the human being bears witness, human beings continuously, throughout their social past, were religious.

And also, we said in the first part that, continuously, the societies of the past, of all races and of all eras, without interruption and without exception, were religious societies. The basis of thought and culture of every society in history was religion for when a historian wants to write about the history of cultures and civilizations and/or teach at the university, we see that his research about the culture of a society or civilization of a nation is automatically transformed into a religious civilization and the recognition of the religion of that nation.

What person can speak about the culture of India without accounting for the spirit, criteria and basis of the culture which is the religion of the Vedas or the religion of Buddha? What person can speak about a culture and civilization which is so ancient like that of China, without studying Lao Tse and Confucius, not as the greatest personalities who influenced the development of Chinese culture, but rather as an axis and cultural spirit of this ancient nation?

We know, then, that human beings, throughout history, were continuously religious. Not only were all societies committed to religion but rather they were based in religion and not only were culture and its spirituality, ethics and philosophy, religious, but rather its material and economic forms and even its urban architecture of the past, were totally religious. As I said, the framework or the mould of classic cities, ancient cities, were symbolic cities, that is, cities built around a temple and the temple was the symbol of the city. Just as today the Eiffel Tower is the symbol of the city of Paris, in the past, the temple was the symbol of a city.

Thus, the historic movement of history founded by the prophets, according to our belief, begins with Adam. That is, it begins with the present day human being and moves towards the Seal. The religion of Islam in its special sense, which is the last Abrahamic religious movement. Now, against what faction, against what thoughts and against what social realities do these prophets arise? What fronts and what factions stood before them (the Abrahamic religions), struggled against them and persevered?

We know that the word *kufr* does not mean lack of religion. That is, the prophets did not come for the people to develop religious feelings and invite them to this. The prophets did not come to invite societies and individuals to believe in having religious emotions and beliefs.

The prophets did not come to propagate worship in human society because the religious feelings, the sense of belief in the unseen, in God and/or gods was continuously within all individuals and in all societies. We do not know of any individual in history who stood against the prophets in the name of atheism or secularism. They stood before theologians or great philosophers or religious leaders, bringing the reasons for the non-being of God or the unseen, but not against the prophets.

In the first place, they (the atheists) had religious belief in another form with another belief. That is, they believed in some sort of metaphysical. Beyond them, there were the secularists, extremely late comers. That is, they relate to an era when philosophy and intellectual thought had grown a great deal in the history of humanity. Separate and exceptional individuals had doubts about religion and gnostic belief but this lack of religious belief never entered the flow of history. It never built a society and its image was never imprinted upon any historic period.

Based upon the introduction which I presented last night, the history of mankind consists of: the history of the multiple human societies in the various social, historic, economic, cultural and religious phases who were all religious. Thus, prophets bring an evolutionary, unified religious movement, based upon the needs and sufferings of their society from the beginning of the history of humanity. They stood against the religion, the guardians of religion and the existing religious beliefs of society. And the forces which always stood against these prophets, interfered with the spread of the religious movement which we believe in and put all of their efforts into destroying or deviating it were the forces of *kufr*, not non-religion.

Thus, religion, in the sense that we believe in, was continuously, throughout human history, in conflict with religion and the mission of the prophets. That is, the main point of their struggle was the struggle with the forces of the religion of *kufr*, not a struggle with non-religion because no non-religious person existed in societies. Rather, it was a struggle with the religion of that society and that time. Fortunately, this word is itself a Quranic term.

Kufr vs. Islam

God says to the Prophet, "Tell the people, tell the *kuffar*,"* - the word *kuffar* refers to persons who have a religion, not non-religious persons. The persons who fought with Abraham, who fought with Moses, who fought in the name of religion against a new religion.

In the Chapter, "*Say to the kuffar*," notice what repetition exists and what accuracy - "*Say (Muhammad) to the kuffar, 'O you who cover over the truth of religion, I worship not what you worship nor worship you what I worship. Nor shall I worship what you worship nor will you worship Whom I worship. Unto you is your religion and unto me is my religion.* ' " (109:1-6)

In these verses, the Holy Prophet is commanded to tell the *kuffar*, the front which is opposing him, struggling against him, "*I wor-*

ship not what you (kuffar) worship." Everything I want to say is in this
Chapter of the Quran.

Thus, the issue is not a question of worship against non-
worship. The issue is that of worship vs. worship. That is, the
people who opposed the Prophet of Islam were not people who did
not believe in worship. They were not people who did not have a
deity. Rather, they had more deities than the Prophet of Islam had.

The issue is about the differences of opinions about the deity,
not about religion. *"I worship not what you worship nor worship you
Whom I worship."* That is that very first terminology but the Holy
Quran repeats its purpose with various terms because of the fact
that it wants to announce it as a principle and fix all its visages and
aspects upon our minds.

"Nor shall I (the Prophet) *worship what you worship."* At the end,
it announces as a cry, a slogan, *"Unto you is your religion and unto me
is my religion."* That is, in history, religion fights against religion.

In the first part, I said that religion, the monotheistic religion,
the religion of *"Unto me is my religion,"* was continuously at war
with *"their religion"*, the religion of those who cover over the truth
of religion. Now who is victorious in this war? It is *"their religion"*
which has been victorious throughout history.

Look at societies. Our prophets, who were rightful messengers
and who we believe in, were not able, in any time in history, in a
perfect way, to develop their religion in a society and realize it in the
desirable form which their religion itself demands.

These prophets continuously were manifested in the form of a
movement, a protest and a struggle against the existing religion in
their own time. History was determined by them (the *kuffar*) and
their religion of *kufr* was the legitimizer of the status quo.

As a result, they remained firm over society. As they had
continuously held the power from the point of view of economics,
from the point of view of social respect and from the point of view
of politics, the religion of truth was not able, of and by itself, from
the beginning of history to the present time, to realize an objective,
external and historic form in a society before them (the *kuffar*) .
Human societies, throughout history, were always under the influence and domination of their religion.

What is this religion and who are these people? The various
names and qualities of these people to whom the Holy Prophet

says, "*Unto you is your religion,*" can be found by studying the religious texts and extracting information about them.

But the religion of the people, as those who are addressed and the religion of God, as the axis, spirit, orientation and invitation, is a religion about which the Prophet says, "*Unto me is my religion.*"

Thus, it is a religion which continuously took the form of protesting against the existing religion and announced a struggle against the existing religion in societies and epochs through the rightful prophets. It is this religion which addressed the people. They have been invited by God, God as He exists in this religion. That is, that which exists in the religion of God and the people, is the religion of monotheism.

For instance, take the phrase, 'God's property'. The word God here does not mean the ancient idea of idolism whereby God Himself would require or need ownership so that some part of what we have should be given to the temple or to the owners of the temple. Here it means 'wealth belongs to God' and God has given it (in trust) to the people.

This interpretation is not mine that I can justify it under he effects of today's way of thinking. This is the interpretation by which Abu Dharr Ghiffari* took Mu'awiyah by the collar and said to him, "You say, 'God's property ' because you want to plunder and devour all of the people's property. You mean to say, 'Property is God's', that is, property does not belong to the people and I (Mu'awiyah) represent God. I will devour all the property. I will give it to whomever I want. I will not give it to anyone who I do not want to give it to."

Abu Dharr made Mu'awiyah understand that God's property means 'the people's property' (that which belongs to the people), that it does not mean that it belongs to the wealthy aristocrats or the insatiable people who live in ease and luxury. It is not the property of special individuals. Rather, it is property which belongs to the people. God is the owner of property, that is, the owner of the property is the people because the people and God are in one front as 'people are of the family of God' .· It is clear that the guardian of the family is in the same front as his own family.

Opposing the family of God, that is, the people, stand the wealthy aristocrats and the insatiable people who live in ease and luxury, individuals who ruled over the people, who always held ownership of the property and wealth of the people and through whom the people were continuously deprived of their social fate, their life and their economic fate.

These wealthy aristocrats and insatiable people who live in ease and luxury were religious. None of them were materialists. None of them were existentialists. None of them were godless. All of them were worshippers of God, even gods. Pharaoh's worship of the gods and his religion is very clear and distinct. The prophets stood before these people in order to destroy them and to destroy their religion which is the religion of multitheism, a religion of the worship of an arrogant leader who rebels against God's Commands.

Just as I said, multitheism is not just a philosophy. It is a religion which promotes the status quo. What was the status quo in history? Social multitheism. What is social multitheism? It refers to numerous races, groups, classes and families in human society. Each family, race and nation had an idol, a god who belonged particularly to them. The worship of these various gods, that is, the belief that society is built upon races, classes, groups and various clans, means each one has their exclusive rights, their own authenticity. Opposition the religion of monotheism through the rightful prophets, that is, the prophets of the religion of God and the people, announced that no creator, nourisher other than God exists in the world and that the Lord is the Creator.

All of the multitheistic religions believed in the creation of God but when it reaches the point of lordship or sovereignty, idols become multiple. Even people like Nimrod,* the Pharaoh, etc. did not claim to be the Creator but rather claimed to be the lord or sovereign of the people. Pharaoh says, "I am your great sovereign." He does not say, "I am your Creator."

The ancient Greeks and all multitheistic religions believe in the Creator. The issue is that of being the owner of the people and then, alongside God Who is the Creator, other gods are made. Why? In order to dominate in various ways, in order to separate humanity and the human race, in order to divide up the unity of human society or a tribal society and a nation into classes and groups which were polarized into the form of ruler and ruled, those who have and those who are abased.

Just as I have said, the religion of God and the deprived and oppressed people throughout history, took the form of a movement which was in a continuous state of struggle and never had the opportunity to develop a society based upon itself (the religion of monotheism). The only and sole society which throughout human history can be said to be or claimed to be or can be recognized as being a society which is based upon this religion, not in the form of a historic reality in one age, but in the form of a symbol, a model, was the society of Madinah.·

The length of life of this society of Madinah was ten years. In the 40,000 years of history of human society, it was only this society which developed to confront the continuous rule of society either indirectly through the name of religion of monotheism or directly in the name of the religion of multitheism. It was only in those ten years that in a city, the economic system, the socio-educational system, the relations of individuals and groups, the relations of classes, the relations of races, the minority and the majority were all based upon the monotheistic religion. After the death of the Prophet of Islam, they were not able to preserve that society with its values and criteria because they could not uproot the ethics inherited from the Age of Ignorance. Thus this organization could not be preserved. We see that after twenty years had passed, the enemies of this movement dominate over the bases of all of this.

Thus we reach this conclusion here by looking at history in this way - religion has opposed religion. With this view of history, all of our judgments, all of the concepts we have of history, of religion, of non-religion, of intellectuals, of the non-religious people of today, and the religious people of the past, the relation between civilization and religion and between the materialist and the religious, change.

In this way, the intellectuals of the 17th, 18th and 19th centuries, especially those of the 19th century who said, "Religion has continuously been the opium of the people," are correct. What religion are they speaking about? They are referring to a religion which existed in history and they analyze that. They see that the religion narcotized the masses of the people. We must say that those who say that religion was a factor to justify the social and economic domination of the minority over the majority are correct.

It is true that this religion in the age of feudalism religiously legitimated the status quo, the enslavement and ownership of slaves. In the society of the age of feudalism, in every form, in every age, in every class, in every shape, when economics ruled in a society, religion was to justify the status quo by misusing the religious beliefs which are based in the primordial nature of people. The examples are many. Look at any corner of history and you will see what religion did there. Take, for instance, ancient Iran and see what religion did there.

Religion in Ancient Iran

The Sassanian era is an era when religion directly ruled over society and even the Sassanian kings and princes were the agents and followers of the high priests, absolute followers of the guardians of the temples. The classes were different, were separate and an individual could not move from a lower class to a higher one no matter what deceit or miracle he made use of.

The First and Second Class

The first class in the Sassanian era consisted of the princes and the aristocrats. The next class was the class of the high priests of the Zoroastrian religion who moved shoulder to shoulder with the first class.

In Sassanian history, sometimes the second class was superior to the first class and sometimes the reverse was true. Both classes were composed of rich aristocrats and insatiable people who live in ease and luxury who ruled over the people, exploited them and kept them abased but the first class, the princes and the aristocrats, did so through coercion and the second class (the Zoroastrian priests) did so through religious legitimation. The wealth of the people was usurped by both of these two classes. Sometimes the wealth of the class of the Zoroastrian priests was greater than that of the class of the aristocrats. In the opinion of one scholar, "Sometimes 18 out of 20 parts of land were in the hands of the priests."

The Third Class

The third class in the Sassanian era were the craftsmen, small merchants, soldiers and farmers. They were the abased masses who were impoverished, the masses whose race is unclean as in India. The third class had no social rights. Even in the 11th century AD, Ferdowsi* says on behalf of Rustam,* "If Islam comes, everything will fall apart. Races will mix together." Rustam said, "Every valueless slave could become king." That is, race and family would no longer be the criteria and axis of the ruler and it would be possible for a slave to come and take over the rule and lead society. This abuse which he made against Islam - the Islam which broke down all of the social barriers - is the greatest honor for us today and it is the greatest slogan of today's abased humanity.

How were these classes legitimated by means of religion in the Sassanian era? The coercive forces, those who, do not know philosophy, do not know how to legitimate religion, do not know metaphysics, resort to coercion. "That shoemaker should not study because if he goes to school, he may become a great teacher. He will then enter the class of teachers and be of a higher class. As his father was born of a man who made shoes, they and their descendants must continue to make shoes even if one of them happens to be a genius. So what if he is a genius. He will have to make use of his genius in making shoes!!"

The Maji Legitimate Class Differences
In the Sassanian era, what do the high priests do? The priests were the people who by means of religion legitimated this separation and this kind of several types of humanities from the point of view of classes. There were three kinds of fire. What is fire? Fire is the symbol and theophany of Ahura Mazda, the great god. Fine. Why three fires? Because in life, Ahura Mazda has three aspects. First there is the fire of Gashasb in Azarbuyjan. Second, the fire of Barzinmehr near Sabzevar and the third is the fire of Istakr in Fars. These are the three fires of Ahura Mazda. But Ahura Mazda also has classes.

The fire of Ahura Mazda which is in Azarbuyjan belongs to the princes and the aristocrats. The fire which is in Fars belongs to the priests and the high priests and the fire which is in Sabzevar and is called the fire of Barzinmehr belongs to the third class.

Even in the religion of Zoroastrianism where the god of beauty and goodness become one, where all people must worship Ahura Mazda and must struggle against Ahriman, we again see that Ahura Mazda does not have one visage in human society, one fire. The sacred fire is itself legitimated to separate these three classes from each other and they are not able to join each other. They are not able to mix together. They do not resemble each other and this separation (from their point of view) is the theophany of the will of Ahura Mazda.

Look at India. When the Buddha wants to speak on behalf of the Divinity or when he wants to express one great feeling, express a progressive thought and give it qualities, he says this method is an Aryan idea or an Aryan thought. Aryan means belong to the Aryan race, that is, it is not from that unclean race which becomes unclean because it is not Aryan.

We see that even for the gods, even for the most sacred of religious feelings and thoughts, the qualities are racial qualities, class qualities and those of family and this continuous separation by means of religion is legitimated because the people of that situation were not based in philosophy.

If they sometimes justify Socrates and Aristotle who said, "A slave develops from the very beginning and a master, master," and Aristotle said, "The noble families who have noble blood are exclusive to these 20 families of Athens and their number will never grow more or less," we can see then that even philosophy was the legitimizer of the status quo. The difference is that when people are influenced by religion, religion, then, becomes the legitimizer of the status quo in the same way as philosophy has been.

It was the religion of the rich aristocrats which was the opium of society. In what form? In the form when it said, "You have no responsibility because whatever happens is the Will of God. Do not suffer from your abasement because in another place you will be rewarded. Don't breathe a word about the contradictions which exist. You will be given ten times over in another world later on." In this way, they prevented the objection, criticism and the inner choice or selection of an individual. That is, the coercive forces and the wealthy took away the right of criticizing, of objecting and the sense responsibility from the people by suppressing the uprising of the people and, at the same time, suffocating this movement, this objection, the criticism, this kind of thinking within the human spirit. How? "That which takes place is something which God wanted. Any kind of objection is to object to God's Will."

Thus we see all of these legitimations are religious ones. All of these are religious, based upon worship, based upon religious belief before that which struggles against religion, a religion which, throughout history, has narcotized, legitimated, deceived. A religion which takes away social responsibility, a religion which legitimates class differences and racial differences, is a religion whose gods are even nationalists.

The gods in Iran were Iranian and the gods in the rank of those the Iranians fought against were non-Iranian. This is in the sense that the gods of the universe are in the higher racial rank of the Iranians who fight against the non-Iranians who are unclean and disgraceful. Who are the non-Iranians? Whoever is not Aryan. We see that religion in this way legitimated the racial situation, the tribal situation and the class situation and the mission of this religion has always been this.

But the religion of the shepherd prophets, the worker prophets, prophets who suffered more than any other class in humanity, who, in truth, directly sensed becoming abased and being hungry, with their spirit and with their flesh, prophets who, according to our Prophet, had all been shepherds, this religion, the religion of these prophets continuously worked correctly against that religion which was from above to below, the religion which was built and spent by the ruling class - which was one with ranks of the ruling class and that of, the high priests.

Multitheism

This religion, that is, the religion of worshipping the arrogant leader who rebels against God's Commands, the religion which in history always ruled and has always been a tool in the hands of the class which had everything in order to suppress and make submissive and silence the class which had nothing, this religion in the Middle Ages took two forms.

One of the two forms of the religion of the worship of an arrogant leader who rebels against God's Commands is very directly and clearly called multitheism as it now exists in Africa. The religion which officially is committed to several gods exists today in Africa. It is a religion which still promotes bright beads and the worship of an animal who is sacred. These types of religions still exist in every primitive tribe.

The struggle against the religion of worshipping an arrogant leader who rebels against God's Commands, the religion of the rich aristocrats and the insatiable people who live in ease and luxury, when it is naked and lives with an open face and is clear, is easy. But the situation becomes dangerous when this religion of worshipping an arrogant leader who rebels against God's Commands and multitheism put on the clothes of the religion of monotheism which is then offered to history in the form of a tool operated by the hands of the wealthy aristocrats and the insatiable people who live in ease and luxury.

This is the second form that the religion of multitheism takes which appears in history. It is here that the religion of worshipping an arrogant leader who rebels against God's Commands in the name of the religion of monotheism struggles against the religion of monotheism. The worship of an arrogant leader who rebels against God's Commands dominates and suppresses the leaders and the sincere worshippers of God and this is dangerous.

In the class of the History of Islam which I teach, I continue to ask one question every year which I have previously mentioned and everyone knows that if this question be answered correctly, many problems will be solved, even social problems.

The question is, "In one society, two persons wanted to propagate one religion. One is Muhammad, peace and the mercy of God be upon him and his descendants, who is victorious and the other is Ali, peace be upon him, who is defeated. Why? The people are the very same Arab people of the 7th century AD. The religion is the religion of Islam. The Quran is the same Quran. The Beloved is Allah. The language is the same. The time is the same. The society is the same and both (the Prophet and Ali) want the same thing but one is victorious and one is defeated. Why?"

A factor must be sought out which did not exist at the time of the Holy Prophet but did at the time of Ali. This factor is obvious. It was the presence of the worship of an arrogant leader who rebelled against God's Commands, the presence of a racial, tribal, family and class religion, the religion of idolism, multitheism, that is, religion had become the instrument for the rich aristocrats and the insatiable people who live in ease and luxury, that is, the Quraysh at that time.

This religion - the religion of multitheism - at the time of the Holy Prophet was clear, straight-forward and direct. Abu Sufyan,* Abu Jahl,* Abu Lahab* were people who officially said, "These are my idols." They directly said, "We have to preserve this house of the Ka'bah because the trade of the Quraysh must continue." .

Mastership and the commercial trade of the Quraysh were connected to idolism. "Our greatness, our position and our respect among the Arab tribes in the world are related to the fact that we are protectors of the house and these idols. These are among our first customs, among our first myths. Essentially, we cannot accept anything else. We are defenders of this." They said these things directly and clearly. A struggle with them is easy. Victory over them is possible. This factor was the cause for the victory of the Holy Prophet.

I will discuss the question through historic and social factors - I am not informed about the unseen - Ali is at war with these very people but these people had found the veil, a covering. What is the veil or *hijab**? The *hijab* is that of monotheism which is put on by those who are guardians of the religion of multitheism. Then when Ali drew his sword, he drew his sword against the Quraysh who were no longer defenders of the idols. Rather, they were defenders of the Ka'bah, people who no longer spoke of preserving customs but rather placed the Holy Quran on their spearpoints and a struggle against this is very difficult.

Now what does this multitheism do? It goes on the *jihad*. It conquers non-Islamic countries. It has a *mihrab*.* It builds splendid mosques. It recites the congregational prayers in those mosques. It recites the Quran. All of the ulama* and Islamic scholars are followers of this, defenders and glorifiers of religious slogans, and it is the slogan of the religion of the Holy Prophet but inwardly it is that very multitheism. Struggling with this religion of multitheism, that is, the religion of enemies who appear in the dress of friends, and a multitheism which fights in the dress of piety and monotheism, against monotheism, is a difficult task. It is so difficult that even Ali is defeated by it.

In all of the history of societies and in social terms, we see that leaders were easily able to run out the foreign enemy and end the racial domination of foreigners when that foreign race and enemy was clearly and directly dominating over the fate of a nation. The arising of these leaders simply and easily defeated the foreign enemy with all of its greatness and worldly glory.

But when these heroes, who had defeated the greatest army in the world, wanted to struggle against those who were the factor causing the bewilderment and difficulties of the nation and society, and struggle with them internally, these very same heroes are defeated. They could not defeat the enemy and these are not just one or two cases. According to Radhakhrisnan, "When coercion and deceit wear the clothes of piety, the greatest tragedy of history and the greatest power of domination over history appears."

Thus when we speak of the religion of multitheism, it must not be imagined that what we mean by the religion of multitheism is a religion which has taken the form of worshipping several things, animals, trees or statues which appeared in the past and then, after being defeated by Abraham and the Prophet, the religion of multitheism was defeated and destroyed. Rather, the religion of multitheism consists of religion feelings of the people, the religious feelings which are in the hands of the rich aristocrats and the insatiable people who live in ease and luxury who always ruled over society.

Thus the intellectuals of the 17th and 18th centuries and the intellectuals of the new era who struggled against this religion, opposed that which is the cause of the bewilderment and the confusion of the people and that which fixes enslavement, disgrace, weakness and the lack of responsibility of the people and protects racial, class and group discrimination in human society, were in the right. Their judgment that religion opposes progress, development, human freedom and equality was correct. Experience later showed that when they put religion aside this judgment was correct.

These intellectuals who struggled for the freedom, salvation and liberation of the people from these superstitions, from these causes of hardship, from the poison of narcosis which they had built in the name of religion and are continuously building (and all the prophets, throughout history, were defeated by them and it was only the prophets who struggled against them in history and no other). Their error - the error of the intellectuals - was an error which exists in the mind of the religious people, as well.

The Intellectuals' Error

The mistake of the intellectuals was that they saw that which history has recorded in the name of religion, worship, in the name of a deity, in the name of *jihad*, in the name of holy wars,the crusades, Islamic *jihad*, as being history and religion and we thought the same thing and still do.

As a matter of fact, as I have said, Islam has a revolutionary notion. It accepts none of these. It believes that the rightful religion and *"My religion..."* will be realized in the future. It does not accept any of those who have ruled people in history under the mask of monotheism or in the name of multitheism in the East or the West.

But the religion which our prophet emphasizes is a religion in which the responsibility of humanity, the responsibility of intellectual human beings and seekers of liberation is like the responsibility of these very prophets of this religion. As the Holy Prophet says, "The scholars of my ummah* are higher than the prophets of the Bani Israel.". And the Prophet said, "The work that our prophets did is work which, after the Seal of the Prophets, must be done by the ulama. The ulama must continue."

The Mission of Muslim Intellectuals and the Ulama

What must the ulama continue? A struggle against a religion for the establishment and revival of a religion. This is the mission: the establishment of a religion which in history was not realized and people have to grow and develop so much so that they find and awaken their consciousness and religious conscience. They have to come to know the meaning of monotheism, come to know that monotheism differs from those who worship an arrogant leader who rebels against God's Commands and the contradictions that exist. They must be able to distinguish the religion of multitheism under the deceitful mask of monotheism and remove this covering of hypocrisy - in whatever form it has taken - throughout the world, tear it apart so that the people attain a religion which is neither born of ignorance - as the materialists say and what they say is correct - nor born of fear.

The Holy Quran repeatedly attacks people who show fear, cry and pray to God the moment a storm comes upon the sea, breaks their ship, causes them to suffer damages and losses but after they are saved, they forget.

This religion is a religion born of fear. This is that very religion which the materialists of the 19th century talk about, a religion which is born of fear of natural forces and even before the materialists said it is born of fear, the Holy Quran attacks the followers of a religion born of fear, the religion of those who use it for transactions, those who worship out of fear, a religion born of classes.

What class created this religion? People who had said, "If you do not have food here, you do not have bread, have patience. There you will be given a table of paradise." This religion is born and developed or built by classes. It is this very religion which spreads like cholera in the religion of our Prophet, in the rightful religion and religions.

It is Ali who calls these religions , the religions of multitheism, 'merchantile religion', 'the religion of those who are afraid'. Thus what worship is the worship of *"My religion..."*? The worship of the liberated. It is the *'ibad al-ahrar*, the religion which is born of liberation, an elevated need, love, the seeking of justice and a movement, seeking of ideals, of human beings, equality, the establishment of equity, the establishment of human justice in the world and the destruction of all evil and disgrace. This religion confronts that religion.

But this religion which guarded poverty, this religion which legitimated poverty - it is true that this religion in history guarded and legitimated enslavement and bondage and held the masses of the people in silence through deceit and narcosis to the advantage of the rich, the insatiable people who live in ease and luxury and the coercive forces. A religion which says, "God has nothing to do with the hunger of this group and the satiety of that one and the bread of this group and the satiety of that one" is a religion in which all religious feelings are transformed into a narcotic state or into the form of an element which seeks isolation and retirement from society and which is pessimistic in relation to material things to the advantage of people who want all material things for themselves.

It is this religion which continuously denies social power, social control, the responsibility of human beings in their fate, their expectations and the physical, spiritual and instinctive needs of individuals, all to the advantage of the coercive and wealthy forces or holds them in a situation which is continuously oppressive in history by means of religious legitimations or by means of the potent and powerful factor of religious spirituality. It is this religion which makes use of hunger, abasement and disease as a sign of God's satisfaction of them and a sign of their preparedness for evolutionary change. It is this religion which opens separate metaphysical accounts for each of its members so that through this means, the assembling of people would be transformed into dispersion and isolation. It is this religion whose religious practices allow all rights to be to its advantage in a society where the people have no right to life, no right to prosperity, no right to ownership and no right to rule. All their rights are made into unkept promises and religion is legitimated to their own advantage.

In no place does the Holy Quran use an extremely harsh tone to crush an enemy of the people except when it speaks of Balaam, that is, the symbol of a person who, throughout human history, distorts the natural primordial and instinctive faith and belief of human beings to the advantage of the prosperous group which rules, which he himself is a part of and to the disadvantage of mankind, that is, the people. When it reaches this point, the Holy Quran puts aside all customary and external explanation and courtesy and says, *"His similitude is like the parable of a dog..."*

What does this tone tell us? It tells us that it is they who guarded and confirmed the wealthy aristocrats (*mala'*) and the insatiable people who live in ease and luxury (*mutrif*), oppression, suppression, exploitation, hardships, discriminations, ignorance and the killing of human talents, throughout history and these pauses, stagnations and killing of great heroes, the killing of great spirits throughout history; it was they who neutralized all of the benefits which should have been gained from the efforts, *jihad* and struggles of the rightful prophets and the rightful religion in history.

Conclusion
Perhaps it will be difficult for you to accept what I am going to say but once you understand, your judgments and views about history and religion will change.

The mission which European intellectuals and seekers of liberation undertook in their struggle with the church, the religion of the Middle Ages in Europe resulted in the liberation of European thought after 1000 years of stagnation. They struggled against this deviated religion and religious deviation, that is, multitheism (*shirk*). They developed a resistance movement against a religion ruled by an arrogant despot who, in the clothes of the Prophet Jesus, rebelled against God's Commands. This mission of theirs was a continuation of that very mission which the divinely-appointed prophets continuously undertook against the reactionary, deviated religion which opposed the people, which opposed human rights, which legitimates or justifies the position of those who hold the power, wealth and/or means by which to deceive, which stupefies and narcotizes people. The European intellectual did this in order to destroy all idols and all signs of the religion of multitheism although they did not explain things in these terms.

This mission, which they undertook rests upon the shoulders of all human beings, now and in the future, who follow the rightful religion. The problem is that they did not distinguish between the two basic religions - human based multitheism and divinely based monotheism.

The religion of multitheism has controlled history so the mission of the divinely-appointed prophets and the religion of monotheism has continuously been blurred, passed over and forgotten. It is the responsibility of every committed, conscious and responsible person to continue the struggle of the divinely-appointed prophets.

It is a progressive movement. It forms the basis for the philosophy of history which, to date, has been usurped by the rich aristocrats (*mala'*) and people who live in ease and luxury (*mutrif*) and their masters in the name of religion.

Our mission is not to return to the past. There is no sense of reactionaryism in what I am saying. Our mission is to continue the mission of the divinely-appointed prophets who were the rightful prophets, who had arisen from the fabric of the people, who were *ummi* and who confronted the pseudo-priests who were attached, affiliated to and dependent upon the rich aristocrats and people who live in ease and luxury, who confronted the self-appointed prophets who were, without exception, from among the aristocrats or the feudalists or who acted on behalf of the princes.

That which the intellectuals of Europe, materialists or rationalists, did not discern about religion just as we have not understood to date is that their conclusion in relation to the religion of multitheism, the religion of history, is correct. This judgment is correct in relation to religions dependent upon the aristocracy and the prosperous classes who abase the people.

But this conclusion and judgment is wrong in relation to religion in a universal sense. The error is that in the view of history, a religion does not exist but rather, religions. This is what Gurwitsch means when he says: A universal society does not exist but rather societies. That is, each society must be studied and judged separately.

Two basic religions have existed in history, two groups, two fronts. One front has been oppressive, an enemy of progress, truth, justice, the freedom of people, development and civilization. This front which has been to legitimate greed and deviated instincts and to establish its domination over the people and to abase others was itself a religion, not disbelief or non-religion. And the other front was that of the rightful religion and it was revealed to destroy the opposite front.

At the same time that I confirm the judgment of the European intellectuals, I believe it to be unfair and oppressive. We can reach conclusions about the religion of Buddha, Zoroaster, Mazdak, Mani and that of the Greek or Roman pantheon which were all attached to, born from and nourished by wealth, power and a class which held itself superior to another: the class of the superior race, the class of owners and feudalists, the class of the materially prosperous and materially successful, the class which dominated.

And if we are objective and honest with ourselves, we must reach another conclusion in regard to the religion of shepherds (Abraham, Moses, Jesus, Muhammad, peace be upon them all), the religion which is more familiar than any other with the anguish or poverty of human beings, the religion, the prophets of which were selected and chosen by God, the real, truthfully selected in history.

How can we objectively generalize and extend the conclusion we reach in regard to a religion (multitheism) held up by dynasties who falsely ruled in the Name of God in the world and a religion (monotheism), the founders and pursuers of which struggled, resisted and undertook *jihad* whereby they were destroyed and their followers were poisoned in prison or killed and massacred by means of those who ruled in God's Name, in the name of a human-based, divinely imitated religion.

These two fronts are not allies. They have continuously opposed each other throughout history. The *jihad* of history has been the *jihad* of the religion of monotheism which says: *"Unto you is your religion and unto me is my religion,"* against a religion which developed so that the hungry will remain hungry, so that others may continue to plunder their bread by rendering people senseless or insensitive to the plight of their fellow human being. How can the conclusion about the latter be the same about the religion which developed and produced an Abu Dharr?

Abu Dharr that pure visage of the perfections of Islam, disciplined by the person of the Holy Prophet, an Abu Dharr who had nothing, neither capital nor literacy nor cultural education, who had nothing, who was under the influence of nothing - who was not translated either - a human spirit, empty of all things.

Whatever he had was produced by this factory of Islam, this Book and this school of thought and action. Abu Dharr says, "I am perplexed by a person who finds no bread in his house. How is it that he does not arise against the people with his sword unsheathed?"

When I mentioned this in Europe and I did not say who had said it, some people thought that it was Proudhon who said this because he spoke more harshly than others." I said, "Proudhon never! He never spoke so harshly." Or else they thought that Dostoyevsky said this. He said, "If a murder takes place somewhere, the hands of the people who did not participate in that murder are polluted as well." What he said was true.

Very well. Let's see what Abu Dharr said. He said, "I am perplexed..." This is a religion which is speaking, not just a religious person. Essentially Abu Dharr has not been influenced by other schools of thought. He did not proceed from the French Revolution but rather he relates to the Ghiffari tribe. He says, "I am perplexed by a person who finds no bread in his house. How is it that he does not arise against the people with his sword unsheathed?"

He does not say, "Against the person who made him poor," "Against the group which exploits." He says, "Against the people." Everyone. Why everyone? Because everyone who lives in this society, even if they are not among those who exploit others, simply because of the fact that they are part of society, that they live in a society in which there is poverty, they are responsible for my poverty and my hunger. How responsible? To the same extent as an enemy is.

That is, he is an accomplice to the person whose exploitation brings about hunger. All human beings are directly responsible for my hunger. More beautiful than this. Abu Dharr does not say, like the UN, "The society which is under pressure, intends to usurp its rights, has the right to arise to attain its rights." Abu Dharr does not say, "You have the right to do this."

He does not say, "You who are hungry have the right to arise against the person who made you hungry." No. He does not say this. He says, "I am perplexed by a person who finds no bread in his house. How is it that he does not arise against the people with his sword unsheathed?"

Is it not unfair, then, and absolute ignorance, ridiculous and, at the same time, does it not make one want to cry, to unrightfully have the same judgment be made about a religion which has such insight in relation to people and the life of the people as the judgement which is rightfully made about a religion which supports hunger in history?

Peace be upon you.

Endnotes to Lecture Two

1. This is the view of some historians but the Islamic view is that man is innately born with the belief in One God or monotheism.

2. According to the Islamic view, Jesus did not die on the corss and will return at the end of Time.

3. That is, the religion of God and the people, the very religion which the rightful prophets throughout history have invited people to join. But as the course of history has always been in the hands of those who directly or indirectly oppose monotheism so that they have not allowed it to succeed, humanbeings must so develop and gain power and consciousness for that religion to dominate over society. They must gain intellectual development and realize human rights to defeat the religion of multitheism and leaders who rebel against God's Commands. The people have never, throughout history, been able to attain a position of power to take the rule from the wealthy and those who live in ease and luxury. Thus the religion of Abraham has never been able to develop a society based on the principles of unity.

Glossary*

Abbas: The clan of Abbas, the uncle of the Holy Prophet, the descendants of whom took over the caliphate in 833 AD from the Umayyids.

Abd Allah: The father of the Holy Prophet.

Abu Dharr Ghifari: One of the earliest Companions of the Prophet, he was born Jundab ibn Junadah from the Ghifar tribe outside of Makkah.

Abu Jahl: A close relative and enemy of the Holy Prophet who planned the foiled conspiracy to kill the Holy Prophet. The Prophet escaped the plot by migrating from Makkah to Madinah in 622 AD.

Abu Lahab: Uncle and enemy of the Prophet of Islam. He is cursed by God in Surah 111 of the Holy Quran.

Abu Sufyan: See Bani Umayyid.

al-kafirun, surah: This is the 18th Chapter or *surah* of the Holy Quran to be revealed. The entire chapter is presented here.

Ali: Son-in-law and first cousin of the Holy Prophet who was selected by the Holy Prophet to succeed him. He became the caliph in 36 AH and is the first Leader (pure Imam) of the Shi'ites.

atheism: See *kufr*.

Badr: This battle of the Prophet against the idolaters was in 2 AH (623 AD).

Balaam: According to a Tradition of the fifth Imam, Imam Muhammad ibn Ali al-Baqir, peace be upon him, the Holy Quran in 7:175-76 is referring to him. Mir Ahmad Ali, in his commentary upon the Holy Quran says that Balaam was a man living at the time of Moses in Egypt who 'knew the greatest name of God', through which everything sought for was immediately granted and it was a very closed secret. The Pharaoh asked him to pray so that Moses would fall into his clutches. Balaam beat a donkey to death in the process of which caused him to forget the greatest name of God and he became one of those who cover over the truth of religion. The Imam says that God made this statement, *"his similitude is like a parable of a dog..."*, a parable for everyone who received guidance from God and yet gives preference to his own indications towards worldly things and follows him.

Carrel, Alexis: (1873-1944). French surgeon, sociologist and biologist who received the Nobel Prize for Medicine in 1912. His writings include *Man, the Unknown* (1935); and *Reflections on Life* (1952).

Commanding to Good and Preventing Evil: *Amr b'il ma'ruf wa nahy an al-munkar.* Ali Shariati defines it in the following ways: That which is described in the language of intellectuals in the world today as 'human and social responsibility', has been accurately described and determined in Islam as commanding to good and preventing evil. (*Collected Works*, Vol 5, pp. 52-3)
***

Islam has not given the 'social responsibility of an individual or a group of its followers, a permanent and determined form in one or several 'social issues' (because a social issue is an unstable, changing phenomenon) but rather, has structured it upon two human institutions which remain permanent in the successive historic ages and changing social forms; it is held in common and is identical in human beings of all ages and all systems. How well is its primordiality shown here. These two are, first, commanding to good or virtue and, second, preventing evil or vice! And we see that these two are two 'tensions of human primordial nature' which Islam has offered its followers in the form of 'obligatory social endeavors'. (*Collected Works*, Vol. 7, pp. 54-6)
***

To command to good or virtue and prevent evil or vice refers to the mission which an individual has in relation to the destiny of his or her society and his or her ideological school which he or she is committed to, that is, the very responsibility of an intellectual, the responsibility of an ideological person, a human being committed to an ideology, a human being attached to a held-back, imprisoned

society.
***

The language of Islam has chosen the language of religion for the social responsibility of its followers which must live through the role of leadership in all historic ages and all social systems and in all of the numerous conflicts and contradictions which bring hardship to people. That is why two general and extremely subtle words, good, virtue and evil, vice have been selected. It has been left to the people to find the areas and examples of each through *ijtihad* (exercising independent judgment based on reasoning), the understanding of the people of each age and each system, depending upon the concepts of evil and good of every land and every age. (*Collected Works*, Vol. 26, p. 205).
***

We must consider and practice commanding to good and preventing evil in its original and extensive Islamic sense because many of the examples of good and evil in society daily take on a new color and a new form and if our concepts of them become fossilized in just a few mental, dry forms in our minds and we only and solely bear a few external examples which are particular to a past age or even to the present one, in a particular system, in this way, with the passage of time, essentially, good and evil would no longer exist. The greatest evil is that we contian the concept of commanding to good and preventing evil in a dry framework of individual and side issues and non-permanent phenomena. And the responsibility of scholarly leadership and the *ijtihad* of the jurisprudents of each age is to determine and discover, through *ijtihad*, the good and evil of their own age and then lead commanding to virtue and preventing vice. (*Collected Works*, Vol. 26, p. 209).

din al-hanif: This is the term used in the Holy Quran to refer to the religion of Abraham and is usually translated into English as 'religion of the upright' or 'righteous' or 'rightful'.

Durkheim, Emile: (1858-1917). French sociol scientist. Among his works are *The Rules of Sociological Method* (1895); and *Elementary Forms of the Religious Life* (1915).

Firdausi: Poet of the *Book of Kings* (*Shahnamah*).

fitrat: Primordial nature. The means through which creation is guided.

fitri: See *fitrat.*

hijab: Muslim modest dress.

idolatry: The worship of gods, deities or idols. It is one type of multitheism.

infidelity: See *kufr*.

jihad: Spiritual and religious struggle in the Way of God.

kuffar: Plural of *kafir*. See *kufr*.

kufr: To deny or cover over the truth of religion and is itself a kind of religion. It is translated as disbelief, infidelity or atheism.

Lat: An idol of the pre-Islamic Arabs.

Magis: Zoroastrian high priests.

maktab: School of Thought and Action. It consists of an assembly of co-ordinated, commensurate perceptions, insights or attitudes of philosophy, religious ideology, ethical values and scientific methods which are built together in one cause and effect relationship, one moving, meaningful form which has orientation, which is living and all of its various parts are nourished from one blod and are alive with one spirit. (*Collected Works*, Vol. 16, p. 11)

Mala': The wealthy aristocrats who are representatives of the coercive forces in society. It refers to people who walk with arrogance and haughtiness.

mihrab: Prayer niche.

monotheism: See *tawhid*.

Mu'awiyah: The son of Abu Sufyan who ursurped the caliphate and initiated the Umayyid dynasty.

multitheism: See *shirk*.

Murji'ites: The Murji'ites were an early Islamic sect developed by Mu'awiyah to propagate for him. They emphasized the suspension of judgment against erring believers and the unfailing efficacy of faith over works.

Mutrif: Insatiable people who live in ease and luxury who accept no religious, human or ethical responsibility for society because their arrogance which is born from their wealth puts them above any sense of responsibility.

Nimrod: Enemy of the Prophet Abraham.

paganism: See idolatry.

Pentateuch: The name of the first five chapters of the Old Testament, also called Torah, the Law. These are traditionally ascribed to Moses and include Genesis, Exodus, Leviticus, Numbers and Deuteronomy.

Pharisees: Jewish rabbis who turned their backs on Jesus and handed him over to the Roman authorities. Whereas another group of Jewish rabbis, the Sadduces, believed in non-cooperation with the Romans and the Zealots believed in insurrection against them, the Pharisees' policy was just like the Murj'ites in later Islamic history: What's it to us or you who is in the right or in the wrong. God will decide on the Day of Judgment.

polytheism: See *shirk.*

Prophet's Caliphs: The rightful caliphs are four: Abu Bakr, Umar, Uthman and Ali.

Quraysh: The tribe of the Holy Prophet, many of whom opposed his prophethood and remained idolaters.

religion: Ali Shariati defines it in the following way: The way from putrid clay (a Quranic phrase referring to the earth from which the human being was created which was mixed with the Divine Spirit) to God is called religion. Religion means way. Religion is not a goal, but a way, a means. (*Collected Works* , Vol. 16, p. 47).

Rustam: The legendary Iranian hero of Firdausi's *Book of Kings,* written in the 10th century AD.

Samaritan: Refers to a magician who was contemporary with Moses and made a golden calf which made sounds of speaking when Moses had gone to Mount Sinai. The Samaritan is referred to three times in the Holy Quran, namely: 20:85, 20:87 and 20:95. Sayyid Ali Akbar Qurayshi in the *Qamus-i-Quran* says that the Samaritan was exiled from human society, that no one was to have any contact with him and he was forbidden to have contact with anyone in any way, shape or form which is required of a social life. This is among the most difficult punishments possible. As a result, he became inflicted with an incurable distemper. This extensive punishment is equivalent to his crime for just as he separated some people from God, he must be separated from people. See Vol. 3, p. 322.

Seal: Refers to the fact that the Prophet of Islam was the Seal of Prophets (*khatam al-anbiya*) and that there will be no more revelation after him.

shirk: To believe in the existence of more than one God. It is translated as multitheism or polytheism and idolatry is one form it takes.

Ta'if: An area outside of Makkah.

taghut: This is a Quranic word which refers to a leader who rebels against God's Commands and refers to Pharaoh.

tawhid: Monotheism. Unity of God. The belief that there is no god but God.

Uhud: This battle of the Prophet against the idolaters led by Abu Sufyan took place in 3 AH (625 AD).

Umayyid: The clan of Abu Sufyan, a man who fought against the Prophet in many battles in an attempt to preserve his own influence and wealth as protector of the idols, was was among the last of the close relatives of the Prophet to accept Islam and, then, only when the Holy Prophet conquered Makkah. His son, Mu'awiyah, usurped the caliphate in 40 AH and began the Umayyid dynasty in Islamic history.

ummah: The Muslim community.

Uzza: An idol of the pre-Islamic Arabs.

Index

Aaron 16
Abbas 29
Abbasid caliphate 36
Abd Allah 29
Abel 16
Abraham 12, 24, 26, 45, 59
Abrahamic religions 22, 25, 29, 37-40
Abrahamic religious movement 42
Abrahamic Traditions 26, 38
Absolute Power 26
Abu Dharr Ghiffari 47, 61-63
Abu Jahl 54
Abu Lahab 54
Abu Sufyan 54
Adam 29, 44
Africa 33, 53
Age of Enlightenment 12
Age of Ignorance 49
Ahriman 49
Ahura Mazda 49
Alberto, Carlos 7
Algeria 6
Ali 8, 29, 37, 54-55, 57
Alid Shi'ism/Safavid Shi'ism 8
Allah 8, 28, 30, 54
Americans 8
Anti-religion 21
Arab people 54

Arabian deserts 7
Arabian Nights 8
Arabs 21, 29
Argentina 7
Aristotle 52
Artist's responsibility 32
Aryan 51-53
Assmann, Hugo 7
Atheism 11, 13, 21
Athens 52
Australia 33
Azarbuyjan 51
Badr 28
Baghdad caliphs 8
Balaam 16, 27-28, 31, 33, 35-36, 58
Balkh 21
Bani Israel 57
Barzinmehr 51
Believers-in-God 7
Blake, William 5
Boff, Cleodovis 7
Boff, Leonardo 7
Bonino, Jose Miguez 7
Brazil 7
Buddha 43, 51, 60
Buddhism 8
Bukhara 21
Caesar of Rome 36
Caesars 39
Caliph 16
Camara, Dom Helder 7
Cardenal, Ernesto 7
Carrel, Alexis 20
Catholicism 7
Chinese culture 44
Christian "liberation theologians" 7
Christianity 7-8

Christo, Libanio 7
Coercive forces 33, 51
Columbia 7
Commanding to Good
and Preventing Evil 32
Companion (s) 32
Confucius 44
Constitution 37
Coptics 31
Costa Rica 7
Day of Judgment 35
Day of Reckoning 15
Day of Resurrection 15
Denying the Truth 23
din al-hanif 11
Disbelief 11. 21
Divine Unity 26
Divine Will 26
Divinely-appointed
prophets 59-61
Divinely-imitative
religion 17
Divinely-originated
religion 17
Dostoyevsky 62
Durkheim 27
Dussel, Enrique 7
Eiffel Tower 44
Europe 9, 33, 59-61
European Christian
intellectuals 11
European intellectuals
11, 59
European socialists 7
Europeans 8, 12
Falsehood, 14
Family of God 47
Fanon, Franz 6
Fars 51

Firdausi 50, 52
France 6, 16
Freedom Movement of
Iran 6
Frei Betto 7
French Revolution 62
Gashasb 51
Ghiffari tribe 62
God 11-17, 20-21, 24-25,
28-31, 38-39, 45-46, 48,
52, 54, 58
God's property 47
Gospels 39
Greece 21
Greek polytheism 7
Greeks 48
Guevara, Ernesto "Che"
6
Gurwitsch 60
Gutierrez, Gustavo 7
Hajj 37
Hereafter 15
hijab 58
History of Islam 54
History of Qum 21
Human responsibility
32
Husayniyah Center 11
Hypocrisy 13-15, 57
ibad al-ahrar 30, 58
ibadu taghut 30
Iblis 15
Ideology 31
Idol-destroyer 12
Idolatry 11, 13, 23
Idolism 24-25. 34. 40, 47,
54
Idol (s) 12-14, 17, 30, 56
India 43, 50-52

Infidelity 11, 21
Intellectual (s) 12, 14
Intellectual's responsibility 32
Iran 8-9, 52
Iranian 12, 52
Islam 6-9, 21, 25, 29-30,50, 54-55, 61
Islamic
    fundamentalism 6
    history 8, 13-14
    Iran 7
    Revolution 6
    society 35
    terms 12
    tradition 8
Israeli tribes 33
Istakr 51
Jesus 12, 14, 20, 24, 28, 35-37, 59, 61
jihad 36-37, 39, 56, 59, 61
Judaism 7
Justice 38
Ka'bah 17, 55
Korah 16, 31
kuffar 45, 46
kufr 11, 13, 21-23, 43-45
Lao Tse 44
Lat 17, 30, 37
Latin America 6-7
Legitimation (s) 15, 21, 30, 34, 37-38
Madinah 49
Magi (s) 33
Makkah 28
maktab 30
mala' 39, 59-60
Mani 60

Karl Marx 6-7
Marxism 7
Marxist socialist 7
Mashhad 20
Mazdak 60
Merchantile religion 57
Message of the Messenger 38
Metternich 28
Mexico 7
Middle Ages 20-21., 37, 39, 53, 59
Miranda, Jose Porfirio 7
Mongols 36
Monotheism 11, 13, 15, 17, 26-27, 30,31, 35-40, 48-49, 54-57, 59, 61
Moses 12, 16, 24, 27-28, 31, 35-37, 45, 61
Mu'awiyah 32, 35, 47
Muhammad 12, 14, 45, 54, 61
Multitheism 11, 13-16, 23-25, 27-37, 40, 48-49, 53-57, 59-60
Multitheists 15
Murji'ites 35
Muslim activists 12
Muslim
    Intellectuals 57
    world 6
mutrif 39, 59-60
Nazism 16
Nicaragua 7
nifaq 13
Nile 16
Nimrod 48
Nishabur 21
Non-religion 21-22, 24,

38, 41, 45, 47
Non- religious 21
Oppressed 7, 48
Oppression 7-9, 31
Oppressor 7, 15
Paganism 23
Palestine 16
Paris 44
Pentateuch 16, 27, 39
People are of the family
of God 47
Peru 7
Pharaoh 16, 31, 48
Pharisees 8, 28, 35-36
Polytheism 11
Preventing evil 32
Priestly function 11-12,
17
Primordial nature 15,
27, 49
Proletarian revolution 7
Promised Land 16
Prophet Abraham 11
Prophet of Islam 14, 16,
28-29, 37, 45-46, 49, 55,
57
Prophethood 14
Prophetic function 11-
14, 17
Prophetic-like 12, 14
Prophet (s) 11-12, 20-22,
29, 34-35, 39-48, 53, 56-
57, 59, 61
Prophet's caliphs 36
Proudhon 61
Psychological idols 12
Quran 7, 25, 27, 36-37,
39, 45-46, 54-55, 57-59
Quraysh 17, 29, 37, 54-

55
rabbis 8, 33, 35
Radhakhrisnan 55
Reformation 12
Religion of revolution 5,
9, 22
Religion of legitimation
5, 9, 31
Religion of monotheism
31
Religion vs Religion 11,
17, 19, 29
Religious
    scholars 12, 14
    spirit 21
Renaissance 12
Resurrection 20-21, 31
Revolutionary religion
30
River Jordan 16
Roman Catholic 9
Rome 21
Rustam 50
Sabzevar 51
Samaritan 27, 36
Sartre, Jean Paul 6
Sassanian era 33, 50-51
School of thought and
action 61
Schopenhauer 28
Seal 29
Seal of Prophets 14, 57
Sebtians 31
Seekers of liberation 59
Segundo, Jean Luis 7
Self 12
Servitude 30-31
Shah 8-9
Shamoon 16

Shariati, Ali 5-7, 11-12, 14, 17
Shi'ism 39
shirk 11, 13-15, 23-24, 30-31
Sign of God 16
Social multitheism 48
Social revolution 8
Social school 31
Socialism 6
Socialist (s) 5, 7
    ideology 6
Socialist Movement of Believers-in-God 6-7
Socio-political idols 12
Sociologist 6
Sociology 6
Sociology of religions 11
Socrates 52
Sorbonne 6
Status quo 11, 30-34, 38, 40, 46, 48-49, 52
Submission 29
Surrender 30, 35
Ta'if 28
taghut 13-15, 29, 39
taghuti 39
Tamez, Elsa 7
tawhid 14, 25-26
Tehran 11, 20
Torres, Camilo 7
Truth 14-15
Tyrannical ruler 13
Uhud 28
Ulama 57
Umayyid 29, 32
ummah 16, 57
Unbelief 21
Unity of God 26

Uruguay 7
Uzza 17, 30, 37
Vedas 41
Versailles 16
Virtues of Balkh 21
Wealth belongs to God 47
Will of God 15, 52
Word of God 7
Yahweh 28
Zoroaster 60
Zoroastrian 33, 50
Zoroastrianism 8, 51